POGO
REVISITED

Containing the complete volumes of

THE POGO POOP BOOK

INSTANT POGO

THE JACK ACID SOCIETY BLACK BOOK

BY WALT KELLY

A Fireside Book   Simon and Schuster

An Up-Front Postscript and Salute to
WALT KELLY
[1913–1973]

"Knowing Walt Kelly was one of the good things that happened in my life," wrote J. P. Mastrangelo in *The Washington Post* on learning of Walt Kelly's death. Multiply that simple statement of feeling by the feelings of his many friends and of his legions of fans all over the globe, to understand how he will be missed.

Bill Vaughan, columnist and Walt's longtime friend, sums up our own thoughts with:

> He was, simply, a genius. The only one I have ever known, in contrast to merely talented men. . . . Aside from his drawing skill, the ideas, the words, the wonderfully playful approach to the English language that came from the unique brain of the Irishman from Bridgeport.
>
> I think he saw Pogo as the symbol of ordinary, decent, gentle people. What he wrote of the possum might well have been about himself: "This is Pogo's home country. He knows it and loves it. He has never had to join anything except the United States of America. . . . And here he will stay, out on a limb a good part of the time, looking innocent, and surviving."

It is with a sense of pride in having been Walt Kelly's publisher that we re-publish this trio of books. We feel that Pogo is immortal and we hope that with this collection the world may continue to enjoy Walt Kelly's wit and satire, to relish his ability to expose good and evil through Pogo and all the wonderful creatures that dwell in Okefenokee, to admire his gift of seeing clearly that "We have met the enemy, and he is us."

THE PUBLISHERS

CONTENTS

THE POGO POOP BOOK

INSTANT POGO

THE JACK ACID SOCIETY BLACK BOOK

THE
POGO POOP
BOOK

FOR JIM BELLOWS
and the others
at the TRIB.

Now, really, how arch
    Can you be when you march
        With a spear,
        With a sword?
You belong

To a curious team,
    You're in the extreme,
        Maybe left,
        Maybe right,
Maybe wrong.

LOW DOWN ON THE TOP
or *The Brothers Grim.*

FUN, like God, is declared dead every once in a while. Every movement—the new left, the new right, the new middle, the new church—should have its own court jester. If he can teach each of the militants to laugh at itself it would be useful, if only for that distant day when there would be nobody else to act as target. The apparent objective of any of these movements seems to be the complete obliteration of all other dedicated thinkers.

The Arab civilization declared a moratorium on thought many centuries ago. Recently it has shown signs of recognizing that others exist with them on this island, even if all the footprints are identified as those of the enemy. However, for many centuries the Arabs were under the impression that civilization, theirs and the only true one, had gone about as far as it could go. So with the right people holding all the right lands, etc., they stamped a staying foot on the status quo. A few hilarious acts worked their way into the criminal code; i.e., a man's hand and a stolen loaf of bread were exchangeable. But for the most part there were few laughs.

The Jews maintained a marvelous sense of humor while they remained free, or out in the open. Unable to find anything funny about Nazi Germany, some of them understandably formed a union, their own nation, and set resolutely and grimly about the business of relocating the herd instinct.

We already know how full of fun Fascists and their counterpart Communists have always been.

Our own nation at this writing is engaged in the grim business of dropping bombs on a country with which we are not at war. Certainly no laughs here.

As our people move in all directions with great grim purpose

16

the safety valve of humor seems to be missing. Humor is not escape. Sleep is escape. Humor is relief. The laugh of finding out the other fellow is funny because he is the enemy is not enough.

Back in the land of 1952 when we found out that any ISM, including Liberalism, is a fraudulent tune played on an off-key instrument, there was a book, *The Pogo Papers*. Its introduction, reprinted here in part, explains what this book is all about too. Here it is, warts and somewhat all:

"Some nature lovers may inquire as to the identity of a few characters here portrayed....Specializations and markings of individuals everywhere abound in such profusion that major idiosyncrasies can be properly ascribed to the mass.* Traces of nobility, gentleness and courage persist in all people, do what we will to stamp out the trend. So, too, do those characteristics which are ugly. It is just unfortunate that in the clumsy hands of a cartoonist all traits become ridiculous, leading to a certain amount of self-conscious expostulation and the desire to join battle.

"There is no need to sally forth, for it remains true that those things which make us human are, curiously enough, always close at hand. Resolve then, that on this very ground, with small flags waving and tinny blasts on tiny trumpets, we shall meet the enemy, and not only may he be ours, he may be us."

---

*Quimby's Law (passed by the town of Quimby after the trouble with Harold Porch in 1897).

SLIDE RULE FOR INFINITY

What kind of a game
　　Where direction's the same?
You run and you race,
　　You wind up on your face---

You slide à la carte
　　And you clutch at your heart,
You're at the right place
　　But you're back at the start.

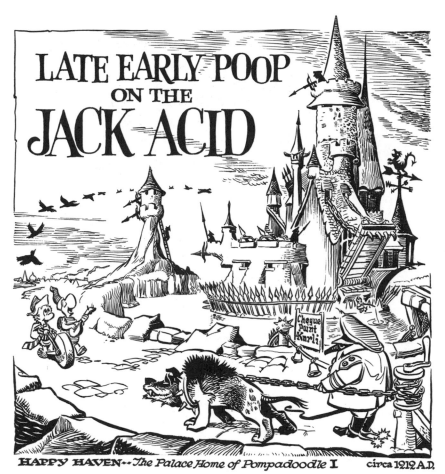

HAPPY HAVEN··· *The Palace Home of Pompadoodle* I   circa 1212 A.D.

22

ALL RIGHT, MEN--WE WANT EVERY **P.R. MAN** TO DO HIS DUTY--- THE SLOVENLY PUBLIC HATES **US** BECAUSE WE ARE A FINE, CLEAN-CUT, HONORABLE PRINCE WEIGHED DOWN BY THE CARES OF OFFICE-- **WE'RE HEAD-OF-STATE** AND THEY HATE IT BECAUSE **THEY** WANT THE JOB---

THEY REFUSE TO WORK IN THE **GARBAGE FACTORY**--- THEY REFUSE TO **EAT** THE GARBAGE--- AND IT IS THE **BEST**--- CRAVENLY, THEY ARE ON A HUNGER STRIKE TO EMBARRASS US, THE **PRINCE!**

THEY HOPE TO **INTIMIDATE US** BY STARVING THEMSELVES TO DEATH! THE **COWARDS!**

AS IS WELL KNOWN

THEY ARE **COMMUNISTS!**

AS IS WELL KNOWN?

AS IS!

NOW, WE WANT THIS SPLENDID GROUP OF MEN HERE TO CHANGE MY--**OUR** IMAGE--- **LET THEM KNOW WE ARE A VERY HUMOROUS ACTOR-- A SONG AND DANCE MAN!** A JOY TO ALL! IN SHORT, WE ARE A **GOOD CHAP!**

24

THERE'S A EXAMPLE OF HIS WORK--- **BEAUTIFUL, HUH?**

NOTICE HIS FIRM GRASP OF "X" "S" AND HIS FINE USE OF "M" AND "V"---ALSO "Z"--- AND GET THAT $G_1^1MbL_ex$! ISN'T THAT **RICH?**

A LITERARY **GASSER!**

YOU KNOW, I THINK YOUR **HAT'S** TOO TIGHT---

THIS GUY IS A **P.R. SHAKESPERE!** HE'LL SHOW US HOW TO BUILD THE **LEADER'S IMAGE.**

LOOK AT IT **THIS** WAY--- IF **40,000** CHIMPS GET OUT **ONE MASTERPIECE-TYPE** WORD OUT EACH, PUT 'EM TOGETHER AND YOU GOT A **40,000** WORD **SYMPHONY!**

EXACTLY! I'M SHOWING THIS TO THE PRINCE!

27

28

31

Ed. note: This, so far as is known, is the only existing accurate version of the origin of the Jack Acid Society. There may be others equally accurate.

34

PREHYSTERIA, A PRIMER

See, see, see Peo·ple! See Peo·ple see, also.

They see Dino·saur! Dino·saur tries to fly.

Peo·ple do not like this. Peo·ple say, "Peo·ple do not

like this. Only birds fly, also only Angels fly also."

"If Gods will us to fly,"
says Chief Stuft-nose,

"Gods give us wigs!"
Stuft-nose means wings.

Chief's nose is stuf-fed.
Chief means wings.

Peo-ple say, "Gods give
us wigs, wigs, yes, wigs!

"Wigs, yeah! Gods give
us wigs! And we fly!"

"Dino-saur cor-rupts!"
cries Mrs. Chief Stuft-nose.

"Dino·saur is evil! But do not stone him! Chase him!

"Do not stone him!" cries Mrs. Stuft·nose. "No stone!"

See! Peo·ple chase Dino·saur! See! Peo·ple stone Dino·saur!

One has Ult·i·mate wea·pon. See! Cool heads pre·vail!

Dino·saur says,"Wiz·ard,   I want to fly. So I wrote
Peo·ple stone me be·cause   a song for them ~~

"To soar! To sing!
Take off! Take wing!
No earth maling·
    ering! A Spring
Harbinger bring
A world to ring.
Such love's the thing,
To soar! To sing!~~

"Will it help them under·   "It", says Wiz·ard,"Should
stand me?"says Dino·saur.   show you are harm·less."

"Funny name for a song: 'TOO SORE TO SING!'~~~

"Need two things to fly: 1. You must try har·der.

"2. (most im·port·ant) yes, 2... I forget Numb·er Two!

"You try Numb·er One; I will try think·ing."

Feast·to·Gods Pic·nic on — Run·way. Ver·y ho·ly...

Run, Dino·saur, run! Oh! See! Peo·ple! Run·way!

"Look, look, I can·not stop," Dino·saur gig·gle·s.

Look, Peo·ple are hap·py to see him. Look!
"So much for Numb·er One," says Dino·saur.

Dino·saur goes to Wiz·ard.
"What is Numb·er Two?"

"Sur·prise!" says Wiz·ard,
"Numb·er Two is *WINGS!* ~

"A lit·tle bird told me. Are
they comf·ter·ri·ble?"

"Oh, yes, oh! Oh, comf·
ter·ri·ble," says Dino·saur.

"Dino·saur is Anti·Holy," say Peo·ple, "He de·stroys Feast!

"We must trap him before he cor·rupts the in·no·cents.

"We'll sac·ri·fice ALL to save Ci·vil·i·za·tion. We'll dig a big Pit·fall on Dino·saur run·way."

Peo·ple fin·ish Pit·fall.
Peo·ple spread Feast-
cloth to hide Pit·fall.

Run! Dino·saur! Run!
Run through Pic·nic!

Peo·ple see Dino·saur run!
He runs! He jumps! He FLIES!

Peo·ple hol·ler a great hol·ler:
"He flies! Dino·saur is a Holy! A Di·vine!

"I say it first!" first-says Mrs. Chief, "He is a Great Di·vine!"

"A Great Div·ide!" cries Mr. Stuft-nose, *with WIGS!*

"A Great Div·ide! You heard it here first," says Chief.

"No! Mrs. Stuft-nose saw Light first," cry many.

Many cry, "We want Wigs to fly!"---"You're not Div·ide!" cry others. A fine re·li·gi·o·us dis·cuss·ion fol·lows.

Many moons later, see! Wizard sees Dinosaur on an Island.

Says Dinosaur,"Wizard! I fly no more. I like it here "Thanks to you I am happy. And I have written a poem:

"Think, beyond Earth,
Lies there a birth?
How high to fly
To pierce a Sky?
Which? Fly or fall
To far of all?
What flash do we?
We fly? We flee?
Look for that star
The shore we are."

"A fine incomprehensile tale," says Wizard, "At home they make war & kill each other very nicely in your Very Name. You gave them something to live for."

It is probably all right to try to be Anything you cannot be when you find that you cannot be Everything that you are---

MacAnnulla '23

44

FREE AS A BIRD

The trouble with birds
   As they flock off in herds,
They're busy at odds
   And they're busy at ends,
They're busy with family
   And busy with friends
And all of their freedom
   Makes whimsical words
Which, wickedly, quickly,
   Is strictly for birds.

She touched me once
  And life then stopped.
She held my hand,
  My frog heart hopped.
She left my mouth
  And formed a smile
With lips that promised:
  "In a while".

I look, I hope, I stand, a dunce---
  Where is the one
    who touched me once?

The KLUCK KLAMS

BUT I FOUND **LIONS** AND **TIGERS** AND **BEARS** AND **GOBLINS** ⋯

I WAS TIRED TRYING TO HELP DADDY GET **FOUND** ⋯ SO I TOOK A LITTLE NAP ⋯

WHEN I WAKED UP, SOME **BABY LIONS** WERE PLAYING ⋯

BUT WHEN I TRIED TO PLAY, TOO, THE MOTHER LION SAID, "IN THAT HOOD, **YOU FRIGHTEN MY CHILDREN** ⋯ **GO AWAY!**"

48

SO I RAN OFF AND THERE WERE SOME **BABY BEARS** HAVING LUNCH.

WHEN I ASKED THEM TO PLAY, THE MOTHER AND FATHER BEAR SCOLDED ME···· **"YOU FRIGHTEN OUR CHILDREN,"** THEY SAID.

THAT MADE ME CRY ···· NOBODY SEEMED TO WANT ME ····
I LOOKED BACK ···· BUT THE FATHER BEAR JUST **SNARLED** ····

IN A LITTLE POOL SOME TIGER CUBS WERE SPLASHING ···
··· WHEN I STOPPED, THE MOTHER LOOKED UP ···

"GO AWAY," SHE ROARED, "YOU FRIGHTEN MY CHILDREN!"

I WAS TIRED AGAIN ··· AND DADDY WAS **STILL LOST** ···
··· **SOMETHING** WAS COMING THROUGH THE TREES.

IT WAS A GREAT GIBBER OF GOBLINS...

THEY DANCED ALL AROUND ME AND KEPT SINGING:

"GO AWAY! GO AWAY! YOU FRIGHTEN OUR CHILDREN!"

I SAID, "MY **DADDY** TOLD ME TO ALWAYS BE **BRAVE.** YOU CAN'T SCARE **ME!**" THEY ALL LAUGHED AND HOOTED···

"BRING IN HIS DADDY!" THEY SCREAMED. AND THEY DID.

"*THIS* **WILL SCARE YOU!**" THEY HOLLERED, AND THEY PULLED THE HOOD AND SHEET OFF DADDY. THERE WAS **NOTHING** INSIDE.

"**GO AWAY!**" THEY HOLLERED AT MY DADDY, "**YOU FRIGHTEN YOUR CHILDREN!**"
MY DADDY WAS JUST **EMPTY**··· **HOLLOW!** I **WAS** SCARED···
··· I RAN AND RAN AND RAN UNTIL I FELL AND SLEPT.

IT WAS ALL A DREAM, YOU KNOW..
··· THEN YOU WOKE AND CRIED AND I FOUND YOU?

YES, I FOUND **YOU.**

COME ON, SON···
IS YOUR HOME THE OLD **DARK HOUSE?**

HOW'D YOU EVER GUESS?

YOU WAIT HERE··· I WANT TO TALK TO YOUR FATHER.

HE MEANS MY **DADDY.**

Mouse into Elephant

Into the city of the Kingdom came Gnot-even, a mouse, hoping to make a protest to the government~~~~

I'M THE ROYAL WATCHDOG, MOUSE ... WHY ARE YOU HERE?

I COME TO PROTEST THAT WE MICE ARE BEING TREATED LIKE A MINORITY!

THE MICE OF THE WORLD OUTNUMBER AND CAN **OUT-VOTE** ANYBODY BUT YOU'D THINK WE WERE A MINORITY GROUP.

LOOK AT ELEPHANTS! THEY'RE A TRUE MINORITY. HOW OFTEN DO YOU SEE AN ELEPHANT UNDER THE BED? YET THEY'RE LOVED BY ALL AND GET THE **BEST** OF **EVERYTHING**...

NOBODY LOVES MICE. ELEPHANTS GET TO LIVE IN BEAUTIFUL FORESTS, THEY EAT **BEAUTIFUL FRUIT.** US MICE HAVE TO LIVE IN HOLES AND EAT WHAT WE CAN **STEAL**... WE'RE AN **OPPRESSED MAJORITY**...

COME ON, I'LL TAKE YOU TO THE CHIEF...

ONE THING THE CHIEF **ABOMINATES** IS AN OPPRESSED MAJORITY... I'M SURE YOU'LL GET HELP...

THE CHIEF'S NAME IS **FRUMP**... FRUMP WILL HELP DISTRESSED MAJORITIES **ANYWHERE** IN THE WORLD.

56

WHAT'S THIS ABOUT AN **OPPRESSED MAJORITY?** WE MUST GIVE HELP, DARLINGS···OH, IT'S **YOU**, DEAR DOG··· WHAT A **DARLING** LITTLE MOUSE··· WHO HAS A SHOT OF KETCHUP?

GOOD MORNING, FRUMP···

I'LL GET A FRESH BOTTLE OF KETCHUP.

THERE'S A DEAR GIRL··· WHAT'S WRONG WITH THAT OPPRESSED MAJORITY? OUGHT TO GET TO **WORK** ON THAT, DARLINGS.

FRUMP IS A POWERFUL FAIRY, SIR, SO DESCRIBE YOUR PROBLEM···

WE MICE ARE BEING TREATED LIKE A MINORITY, SIR···ER··· MADAM, AND WE ACTUALLY ARE A TRUE MAJORITY, WHEREAS, **ELEPHANTS**···

59

IT'S STARTING TO RAIN!

GNAWSEA, DEAR, WHY ARE YOU OUT IN THE RAIN?

THE HOUSE GOT **SMALL**···

ALL OF A SUDDEN EVERYTHING STARTED TO **DWINDLE**··· THE WALLS **CLOSED IN**··· THE DOORS **SHRANK**··· I COULDN'T **BREATHE**···

I JUST BARELY MADE IT OUT THE DOOR···WHAT **TERRIBLE** THING HAS HAPPENED? WE HAVE NO PLACE TO **LIVE.**

ORG

AND LOOK INSIDE···**ELEPHANTS!** TINY ELEPHANTS··· THEY RAN IN FROM THE **ZOO** WHEN IT STARTED TO RAIN···

THEY'RE DANCING AND PLAYING THE CHILDREN'S BANJO···· THE PEOPLE **LOVE** THEM···THEY NEVER LOVED **US!**

OH, THEY'RE FEEDING THEM CHEESE SOUFFLÉS, PINEAPPLE TARTS, COCOA WITH MARSHMALLOWS···

AND NOW IT'S *SNOWING!* THIS IS TOO MUCH!

FOR THE SAKE OF MY FAMILY AND MY NERVOUS STOMACH, I'LL COMPLAIN TO FRUMP···

I'M PICKETING YOU, *FRUMP!*··· YOU ARE A DECEITFUL MEGALOMANIAC! YOU HAVE TAKEN ADVANTAGE OF A DEFENSELESS, PITIFUL MAJORITY AND PUT US OUT OF OUR RIGHTFUL HOME!

I ORDERED SNOW TO COOL THINGS OFF··· *WHAT'S WRONG?*

HELP!

EVERYTHING IS WRONG ··· THE ELEPHANTS ARE LITTLE AND CUTE··· EVERYBODY LOVES THEM ···

US MICE ARE OUT IN THE STREETS IN THE SNOW··· WE WANT OUR BIRTH RIGHTS OF FREE FOOD AND LODGING RESTORED!

I HATE TO SEE A GROWN MOUSE CRY!

EVERYTHING I'VE DONE TODAY HAS **BACKFIRED**... VERY WELL, I'LL **CANCEL** THE **SNOW** AND CHANGE **EVERYBODY** BACK TO HIS **RIGHT SIZE**...

RAGOUT A LA CARTWHEELS!

WHISHT

HA!

BOO! DO YOU HEAR? BOO! BOO?

HEH!

COMFY, HONEY?

THAT'S THE WAY IT IS, DARLING --- WE CAN **ALWAYS** DELIVER A **MIRACLE** --- BUT WOULD WE WANT TO LIVE WITH IT? I COULD CLEAN UP THIS ALLEY, BUT HOW WOULD WE FIND OUR WAY AROUND IN THE **DARK**? NOW THE MOUSE CAN GO BACK AND **EKE** OUT A **LIVING** --- *SAY, I LIKE THAT!*

I ALWAYS HAVE.

67

THE
COMPUTER-COMMUTER

A TRAGEDY

Being the partial and impartial history of Chester Pott,
a humanlike computer,
constructed by a fiendish, mad scientist
who hoped to enslave his creation
but was thwarted by Chester who in turn came to a sad end
through falling heir to the ills of the flesh
in the big city.

PERHAPS you have wondered over the years why most scientists who invent inhuman devices or human machines are usually described as "mad." The reason they are mad is that they have such a devilish time nailing their inventions together. Each keeps hammering himself on the thumbs. And, inasmuch as such a genius is all thumbs anyway, this gives him a lot to be mad about.

Coleman the Calm was that kind of man, and he got so mad at the workaday world that his own brain finally outsmarted him. Coleman detested commuting to the city to work in the marketplaces.

"It is bad enough being a human computer in the market," said Coleman, "without also having to be a human commuter to boot."

And Coleman *was* booted, quite regularly, off the train for being nasty to his fellow passengers and to innocent trainmen. "I shall invent a machine that will commute for me and then go to the market and compute for me." He grinned at his seat companion, a four-year-old stranger who seemed to be covered with chocolate. "You know, it will be a kind of inhuman machine," he confided.

The stranger licked thoughtfully at his elbow for a moment and then observed, "I see, sir, a sort of self-portrait?"

Coleman the Calm fetched the tad a cruel blow across the chops with an umbrella which he carried for the purpose and was promptly thrown off the train by his enraged fellow commuters, all of whom had been splashed with chocolate.

Undaunted, Coleman rose from the railside marsh grass on the outskirts of Utter Bliss, N. J., and raced the thirty-two remaining miles to his home, chuckling as he ran and eating the remainder of the child's candy. You could put Coleman off, but you couldn't put him down.

At home Coleman went feverishly to work. Dismantling a coffeepot, an old coffee grinder, an unemployed cash register and a set of Christmas tree lights (which he had beaten to death in a rare holiday spirit when they refused to work), he quickly laid out the bare bones of a working computer. He went to bed happily, sucking his sore thumbs and rousing only intermittently to utter a sharp cry of outrage at the hammer on the floor.

Next morning the new inventor whacked his computer together
in a fury and strapped roller skates to its stubby legs. Then he
pushed it down the hill to the railway station, bought it a commuter's ticket book, fed it instructions for the day at the market,
along with directions on how to get to the market and return.
With that he said, "Good luck, Chester," whacked Chester on
the back and put him on a handy train.

"Who was that?" asked Norman Nervous, the popular stationmaster. "He looked like a coffeepot."

"He comes from a long line of Potts," said Coleman, and went
home.

When Chester Pott returned that evening, his little drawer that came out at about belly-button level was stuffed with money. "There would have been more," he explained to an astonished Coleman, "but I got hungry on the way home in the train. Must have eaten a couple thousand dollars' worth."

"You what?" exclaimed Coleman the Calm, jumping up and down and belching. "You ATE two thousand dollars' worth of pure MONEY?"

"Naturally," said Chester. "That's the way you built me. To be fed paper. Remember? Hand me a slice of that dictionary, will you?"

Absentmindedly Coleman pushed the whole dictionary across the table and then went back to counting the money that Chester had dumped before him. "There's $18,644.76 here," he said, looking at his brainchild with round eyes.

Chester rubbed his front. "Brother," he grunted, "you can have that hard stuff. I tried the other 24 cents. Pure heartburn. A guy could get the DT's on that junk. No more hard stuff for me." He bit off everything back to *N* in the Webster's.

Suddenly Coleman looked crafty. "Tell me," he purred in a kindly rasp, "where did you get cash like this? The market pays off differently. Credits, shares, that sort of thing, but not cash. Where'd you get it?"

"A fellow in the Exchange saw me clean up a couple hundred thousand in credits, et cetera, and he met me outside," Chester explained. "It was a pretty slim bundle of paper that I had, I can tell you. He was very kind. Offered me $26,445 for the lot. A *much* bigger bundle of paper."

Coleman the Calm gave a screaming groan and fell over backward into the fireplace. Chester pulled him out and watched his hair smolder with some curiosity. Then he ate the rest of the dictionary.

It was quite dark outside now. Chester was fascinated by this darkness. All he had seen of Utter Bliss, N. J., had been such parts as were visible by day. It's *got* to be better in the dark, thought Chester, and he skated out the door.

The metropolitan section of Utter Bliss was wrapped in a sleepy quiet. The post office was quiet. The railway station was quiet. Norman Nervous was not quiet. He was asleep and snoring right across the tracks from the firehouse.

In the gloom, near the firehouse, a small figure stood on the curb. It looked just like one of the things that Chester Pott had discovered were girls while in the city that day. The curious computer skated by in a swirl of heavy pirouettes. "Good evening," he offered, tipping his percolator lid. There was no answer.

"I wondered if that horrible noise from over at the station was bothering you," said Chester, circling on one skate. Again there was no answer.

Pott thought again. He was not sure of girls. Maybe this one would enjoy a spin through the evening, a roller-skate ride in the country. He cleared his throat and removed his percolator lid.

At this moment, over the corner of his nose, or spout, Chester saw something moving up in the night. Clearly it was one of those things mentioned with the rest of the words he swallowed when he ate the dictionary. It must be a wild beast. To confirm this conclusion, the figure by the curbside seemed to flinch. It gave a little squeal. The beast kept coming on. Directly toward them. It seemed headed for the girl.

Chester's computer brain raced. He summoned up words but half digested. "*Avast, you mongolian blackleg! Begone, you pariah cur! To the hills with your sniveling mannerisms!*"

The beast hesitated. Pott aimed a mighty kick at it, intending to split the monster in twain. Chester's other skate was not ready for this. He did a stunning loop and fell at the ogre's nose with a crash that momentarily halted the pinochle game upstairs in the firehouse.

I'm dead, thought Chester. My lifework over in less than a day. He looked up, but the beast was departing. Pott was not to be eaten this time. "What kind of fierce wild beast was *that?*" grunted the computer, trying to get upright.

"A dog," explained the figure. "Here, lean on me to steady yourself."

Pott clawed and fought his way up. "My," he exclaimed, "you're quite cold!" He held on to the unmistakably feminine form perhaps a trifle longer than necessary.

"I know," came the reply. "I'm always cold. I'm a fireplug."

The Computer's brain raced again. Fireplug, he remembered. "FIREPLUG: —A hydrant. (GR. *hydro*—water) *n*. A discharge pipe with valve and spout…" Pott ceased remembering. "Cheese!" he blurted out. "I thought you were a girl!"

"I am. A girl fireplug." She paused and then sighed, "Not many of the fellows stop to talk. Not without being led away. And *nobody* has ever rescued me from a fierce wild beast before. You're very strong and brave. What's your name?" She hesitated. "Mine's Veronica."

"*My name is Chester Pott!*" cried the Computer with a sudden wild exuberance, and he gave a mighty leap into the air. Chester stayed down longer and was at least twice as long in getting to his skates this time.

For the next few weeks Chester Pott went into the city every weekday, brought back money every evening and visited Veronica every night. He was in love with a fireplug and tried to make up a song, but he had difficulty with a rhyme for "Veronica."

Coleman the Calm buttered his burned scalp and remained indoors counting his money and his blessings. Each night he wound Chester up and recharged his batteries. In an unusual burst of benevolence he subscribed to every newspaper in the country so that Chester would have a varied fare. Pott became very fond of Chinatown newspapers and *Il Progresso*. He complained, however, that the former didn't stay with him very long and the latter repeated on him.

"You're an ingrate," growled Coleman as he stuffed money behind the walls. The attic was filled. Coleman no longer asked his computer-commuter how much money he actually made at the market. He couldn't bear to balance the take-home pay with the actual earnings.

The last time the two had a discussion about the cash, Coleman was relieved to find that Chester preferred the uplift of the *Christian Science Monitor* to plain bills. "I don't really care for the taste of money anyway," mused Pott. "Except for the thousand-dollar notes. They're delicious. But there's never too many of those. A mere handful." Coleman groaned and never brought up the subject again.

There came a night when Veronica asked what Chester did in the city. "I make money for Coleman the Calm," replied Pott. "He puts facts and figures into my craw, I digest them and come up with the right moves to make on the Big Board. Then I collect the winnings, turn them in for cash, and go home on the train. It saves Coleman from being his own computer-commuter."

"Why give Coleman the money?" asked Veronica. "He's cheating you. It's you that's doing the work and all the thinking."

"You're right," said Chester. "I never did like him. Besides, lately I'm so high on paper that I can't remember what he feeds me in the way of facts and figures. So I just guess when at the market. It works as good as anything."

"You ought to cut down on the paper, Chester," said the lady fireplug. "Just a couple a day. Then have one with me when you come home. You have a pulpy look and you have ink on your breath all the time."

"At least I move around," said Chester with annoyance. "I don't sit in a little town in one place doing nothing."

They parted without so much as an angry "good night." For the first time in his short life Pott wished he had a door to slam, so he lifted the lid of his computation gear and banged it down. It hurt.

Immediately things go from bad to worse. Chester stays in the city the next night. He puts away the contents of a trash basket and starts an unsteady conversation on a street corner with a lady who shares his taste for the big life. Within an hour he has fed her all the day's proceeds in large bills. Too late, she laughs cruelly and identifies herself as a Government agent, a mailbox.

"You will have to answer to the Internal Revenue people now, big boy." She laughs cruelly again. "Ta ta."

Heartsick, betrayed, Chester skates slowly to the train.

Back home, Coleman the Calm is waiting. "So," he says. "Look at the condition you're in. I can guess what happened. Just for that, your supper goes in the fire."

"No," cries Chester, but too late. The bundle of direct mail, catalogues and comic books is thrown into the flames. In a rage Coleman hurls the evening papers in also. There is a flash of fire. Coleman stumbles back. Chester skates to the door in panic. The rug is burning. The table glows and explodes in flames. Coleman, his new hair smoking, claws at the walls. "My money, my MONEY!" he cries.

The computer screeches outside and down the street. He skates straight to Veronica. But there a terrible sight meets his eyes. Veronica is surrounded by men in funny hats and raincoats. Each has an attachment for Veronica. Pott is dismayed and then horrified at the things they do to her as they pour Veronica's lifeblood on the fire. It is all for naught. Coleman the Calm races from the structure clutching a few charred thousands, but the house is destroyed.

Later, completely disillusioned, Chester skates glumly past the fireplug. "If you're going to fool around like that, baby," he growls, "I got better than you in the city."

"I thought as much," hisses Veronica. "You're like all men. You have fallen heir to the ills of the flesh in the big city."

Chester stirs his great computer brain and tries to remember a line from Verdi meaning women are fickle. "I got it," he mutters. "*Funiculi, Funicula!*"

"The same to you with lumps," says the lady fireplug and falls with a gurgle into a steely silence.

The next morning Norman Nervous stood on the station platform looking down at the motionless form of the computer-commuter. "It's a machine that Coleman the Calm called Chester Pott," he explained to the fire chief. "He had it rigged to take the train, go into the city, do business for him and return. A computer—automated, you know?"

"No wonder it knocked off. Look, it's got a whole bundle of the Sunday *New York Times* stuck in its craw," said the chief. "How do you *start* a thing like this?"

"It ain't how it starts, it's how it winds up."

And Coleman the Calm was not telling. He was through. He took the slightly burned money he had left, bought a life residence in a dog kennel and spent his time eating gravel.

To this day, when Utter Bliss commuters ask Norman Nervous how to start the machine, the stationmaster can only repeat: "It ain't how it starts, it's how things like this wind up. That's what beats *me*."

Beats *me*, too.

THE PUSH-BUTTON WORLD

Hail to the hippity push-button world,
The jolliest roger we ever unfurled,
With buttons to summon whatever we need,
With buttons for giving and buttons for greed
And buttons for mackerel and buttons for cod
And buttons for loving and buttons for God,
Maybe buttons for thinking and dying will send
A finger for pushing the button for END.

REQUIEM FOR
AN EXAGGERATED OBITUARY

In the beginning
   Who was alone?

In any ending
   Who is unknown?

In the beginning
   There was a friend.

In the beginning
   There was the end.

Whose GOD Is Dead?

Chicken Little, the noted theologian, was in a ferment. His busy little brain had finally figured out the answer to a religious question unsolved for centuries---

SEE THERE, GENTLEMEN? MY CALCULATIONS PLACE THE NUMBER OF **ANGELS** WHO CAN DANCE ON THE HEAD OF A PIN AT **2,619½!**

BY JING, HE'S **RIGHT!** IT DOES SAY **2,619½** RIGHT THERE IN **BLACK** AN' **WHITE!**

WHAT IS A HALF AN ANGEL?

YOU QUESTION **MY** WORD, SIR?

NOT AT ALL, DOC--- BUT HOW **BIG** A PIN IS THIS?

94

95

WORD TRAVELS **FAST**--- THE KING FOUND OUT THAT GOD WAS DEAD--- SO HE HASTILY APPOINTED A **NEW ONE** AFTER AN AGONIZING, APPRAISAL--- LOUIE, THE LARK, OUR NEW GOD.

HOW COME?

Louie happened to fit the cage---uh--- Church we had---

Now He's ever to be in Church where He belongs--- Where He can ever sing praises ---and I will write the words.

I THOUGHT **I'D** WRITE THE **TUNE**, KINGIE.

BUT **HOW** CAN YOU DO THAT?

Simple! First, you found a church, then you find a God that fits it---

If it turns out that the God doesn't fit in a while--- **BOOM!** He's dead and you advertise for a new one.

100

101

GOD IS NOT DEAD

He is merely
unemployed...

INSTANT
POGO

This book is for S<small>TEPHANIE</small> W<small>AGONNY</small> K<small>ELLY</small>,
a good club fighter at all weights.

A WORD AT THE START

YOU TAKE A PINCH of possum and add hot water. Then you've got instant Pogo. Inasmuch as most possums spend most of their lives being dead, asleep, or moodily eating lettuce, new corn, and garbage (possums being both spoilers and mop-up artists), the hot water is needed to change the ordinary American marsupial into a tiger.

Pogo is at his most interesting when he's in hot water. That is why he reluctantly finds himself at odds with all extremists. As he has said, he's against the extreme right, the extreme left and the extreme middle. A possum no less than any other man is judged not by what he's for, but what he's against. It may be that it is physically impossible to be against the middle but there are many enemies in the strata to consider, including the muddlesome bore.

Naturally, if you are against either extreme, you are thought to be in the middle, which is no place to be when the latest philosophical fad tries to sway your sense of direction. It is probably folly to try to fight all three entrenchments. And these positions are trenches indeed, for each can eventually become the tiresome stuff of reaction. Freedom joins no organization but remains the goal toward which all organized men must move. But if it is folly to fight all reaction, it must be remembered that fools take many disguises, not the worst of which is that of the cartoonist.

To quote from a TV broadcast I made recently for CBS, "TV Views the Press," "Satire, in the hands of most cartoonists, including this one, becomes, at best, sarcasm—at worst, ridicule. This is especially true of editorial cartooning, but it is also true of the comic strip, where pathos, buffoonery and unadulterated malarkey make up the daily grist. On occasion we come close to satire

107

through parody, which is merely broad caricature both in words and in pictures.

"Being a parodist and buffoon I was surprised recently to find the cartoon of the pig accused of being satire in bad taste. Also, POGO was accused of having gone in for editorial comment and of making fun of politics. The accusers were editors of a few papers carrying POGO who thought they saw in the pig some resemblance to a head of state. (The papers objecting were in Japan and Canada.) If editorial comment, whether on social themes or political, is ruled not part of comic strips, it may account for the low level of entertainment seemingly demanded by the objecting editors. If politics is not a matter of fun, what's the use of the practice?

"We [cartoonists] might come close to parody, perhaps unwittingly, in our search for fun, but true satire is beyond us. When you deal with fifty million readers every day you don't monkey around too much with subtlety, especially in the space provided [in newspapers] for strips these days. It must be remembered that satire is a subtle science. Nothing that we have done reminds me in the least of Anatole France's *Penguin Island* or of the Reverend Dodgson's *Alice in Wonderland*."

Another quote, from Bill Vaughan of the Kansas City *Star*, a man who has been trying to divine Pogo's identity and position for years: "If, by possums, Kelly means ordinary decent gentle people, that's his business . . . the Pogo political position is sometimes a little hard to pinpoint . . . my impression is that [he has] always stood foursquare on the side of gentleness. . . ."

After such a bouquet, it may be that the house has emptied, but for those members still present, particularly if they are gentlefolk in Japan or Canada, the banned strips follow.

WALT KELLY

THE ENTRANCE OF THE COMEDIANS

In which livestock is added to the broth of the boys ···

FATHERLAND!

¿Qué es esto? ¿Jabón? YOU SAY HERE IS NO SOLDIERS···· ¡Venga! YET YOU HERE TO INSPECT···· NO? ¡Espere un minuto!

BUT I SAVE THE U.S. TROUBLE"··· I COME TO SEE·· THEY DON'T HAVE TO TELL.

AND I SAVE THEM TROUBLE WITH MY SOLDIERS, ТОВÁРИЩ! THEY DON'T HAVE TO COME TO MY COUNTRY TO COUNT··· I'LL TELL ALL···EVERYTHING··· EVERYTHING I CAN REMEMBER ···THO' MY MEMORY IS SHORT.

····IS GOOD TO EAT WITH FRIENDS; THE BREAD OF STRANGERS CAN BE VZЯЧ HARD. DID YOU BRING ANY LUNCH?

¿Qué es esto? ¿Carne? No·· ¿Qué es? ¿Bananos? No··· ¡Es puros!¡Cigarros! ¡Sí!¡Es tabacos! YES, IS HERE THE CIGARS FOR THE LUNCH, SI!

CIGARS?! FOR LUNCH?

IN MY COUNTRY THESE IS LUNCH! LIKE FRIJOLES! ¡y azúcar! YOU LIKE WITH SUGAR, SI?

ONE THING MY COUNTRY GOT LIKE THE DICKENS! IS SUGAR! ¡y tabacos! ¡Hoy! THESE ONE THINGS WE GOT! ¿Cuanto? ONE LUMP?

111

112

THE ECONOMY OF THE U.S. WILL GO *PFOOT* LIKE THAT... MARX MY WORDS.

I TAKE NOTES, HOKAY? HOW YOU SPELL THESE *PFQOT?*

WITH A BIG FOOF... NOW, MARX SAID IT, SO BE IT... I TAKING OUT THESE TRADE STAMPS... PUCE STAMPS.

THESE WILL DO THESE...? UPSET THE KENNEDYIAN APPLE CORE?

NOT *CANADIAN*.. U.S. APPLECART! THESE ARE FAKE... THERE ARE NO THING BEHIND THESE TRADE STAMPS, NYET?

¡Perdóneme! THESE STAMP SHOULD BE IN *MY* COUNTRY... SOMETHING IS IN BACK FROM *EVERYPERSON* THERE....SI! THE MAN WHO FOLLOW YOU IS FOLLOW BY SOME PEOPLE WHO IS FOLLOW BY ETC.! *¡Estoy enferma!*

DA DA DA

ECONOMICALLY, WE CAN RUIN U.S. ALL LEGAL ACCORDING TO COMRADE KARL, AS IS WELL KNOWN LIKE GOSPEL, GOSPODIN!

¡Y! WITH THE COUNTERFEITS TRADE STAMPS! I WOULD HAVE DO NOT SO, NO!

I WOULD UNLEASH los soldados OF MY COUNTRY! AND THEN IS mucho malo, *VERY BAD,* FOR THESE NOW WHAT YOU CALL U.S.y A. SI! SI! SI!

BUT I READ IN BOOK BY MARX.... MAKE THEM *SPEND, SPEND, SPEND!* SO WE FORCED *THEM* TO SPEND BY STARTING YET A *SPENDING* RACE".HO HO!

I NO READ THESE BOOK BUT I GET THE PICTURE...

LIKE ALL THOSE RACE YOU IN.... YOU ARE WIN *THESE* ONE, AMIGO, MY PAL?

HO? HO? DA! WE WIN EASY.... WE *BURIED* THEM ....

WE WENT BROKE *LONG AGO.*

HIS EYES, HOW THEY TWINKLED

❦

In which the dotting of the teas matches the crossing of the eyes...

BIG RUSSIAN PROVERB: IN THEATRE, TO BRING DOWN HOUSE, KNOCK PROPS OUT. *HO? HO?* NOW TO UNDERMINE ECONOMY... SO...

THESE PEASANTS BUY GROCERIES AND GET STAMPS... THEY SAVE 'EM, TURN IN THEM AT **REDEMPTION STORES**... FOR THIS THEY GET QUICK, LIKE SO, YACHTS, SABLES, AIRPLANES, VACATION TRIPS, POTS AND **SPITTOONS**...

TRACTORS, PERHAPS?

THESE THINGS THEY WANT... *NOT THE RICE, BEANS, CHOCOLATES, PIES, MUTTON, PORK, BEEF, CHICKEN, BANANAS, FRUITS, SUKIYAKI, STROGANOFF AND PROSCIUTTO* THAT THEY *BUY!*

¡Espere!

¡Pare! Amigo, YOUR ELOQUENCE BRINGS TEARS TO THE EYE OF ONE WHOSE HEART BLEEDS FOR THE EMPTY STOMACH OF A NATION... I, MYSELF, ONCE MISSED A MEAL.

SEE, OUT WE PUT COUNTERFEIT PUCE TRADING STAMPS... THE PROLETARIAT WILL **SAVE THEM,** THE CAPITALISTS WILL **REDEEM THEM** ...

115

HO, MY FRIEND *POGO!* MEET MY GOOD FRIEND, WHAT'S-HIS-NAME, HH···· YES, *FIDO*···· NICE GUY, NYET?

IS VERY FUNNY STORY ABOUT HIM, IS FUNNY IN *RUSSIAN* OR ENGLISH ··HƎ IS LƎꓭꓵИIИG ƎИGLISꞮ bꓴ ꓭꓭꞰƎИ RƎCỖꓭꓷS ~~~

SỖ ꞱƎ IS SPƎꞰIИG ꓭꓭꞰƎИ *ƎИGLISꞱ!* HO HO HO HO HO HO! *IS FUNNY?*

YOU KEEP *THEM* KINDA *JOKES* COMIN' INTO THE COUNTRY AN' ALL DEALS ON A LOWER *TARIFF* IS *OFF*···

es SMART FOR YANQUI, NO?

IS FRIGHTENED LOOK ON YOU, POGO, WHEN YOU DISCOVER HERE WE ARE? *NYET?* DA, DA!

MY NAME AIN'T *POGO*····

WHY DO YOU DISAVOW IDENTITY, COMRADE? YOU ARE MEMBER OF *APPARATUS?* THE C.I.A. MAYBE?

DON'T B'LONG TO NO *UNIONS* NEITHER.

IS A FUNNY PROVERB IN *RUSSIAN* ABOUT FEAR: DỖИ꓅ ꟿORꓭꓹ, Ꟑ̈ỗꟃ CꓯИ'꓅ DIƎ ꞴƎꟃOꓭƎ YOꞱR DꓱƎꓯ꓅Ʇ····*HO HO?*

HILARIOUS

THERE *SHOULD* BE A HIGH TARIFF ON RUSSIAN JOKES···· YOU'LL BE PUTTIN' OUR GAG MEN OUT OF BUSINESS.

A NEW WAY TO UNDERMINE *ECOMEDY* ?

THE CAREFUL CHARGE

It is best to run softly and carry the big stick ··· away?

WHEN WE ARE GOING TO UNDER-MINE ECOMEDY OF U.S.? ¿Domingo? ¿Mañana? ¿A qué hora?

CKÓPO! QUICK! LIKE FLASH! BUT FIRST THE PLANS MUST PERFECT.

YOU HAVE MUCH BIG TALK, AMIGO MIO! YOU BIG WITH WORDS ·· BIG WITH PROMISE! SMALL WITH RESULT! WHAT YOU GOT? ONCE MORE, FIVE YEAR PLAN? I NO GOT FIVE YEARS.

BE PATIENT! I CAN SEE YOU NOW, REWARDED BY BIG JOB··· WE GOT OPENING···· A SPOT TO FILL···· ON LENIN'S RIGHT HAND! HOW YOU LIKE?

SOUNDS GOOD, SI····

HOW COME IS THESE JOB OPEN, CHICO?

THE LAST COMRADE QUIT···· YOU'D LOOK GREAT IN THERE, SPORTS.

119

I dunno, Molester, all this tough talk by the Jack Acids gives me pause---

YOU FORGET, ALL EMBRYO SOCIETIES HOPING FOR SOCIAL GAINS FOR THE MASS MUST REVERT TO RUTHLESS *METHODS* AT THE START··· NEVER SPARE THE ENEMY, DEACON.

VICKSBURG

PAT CASHMAN

YES, IT IS A SAD SOCIAL TRUTH, ONE WHICH THE **REDS** UNDERSTAND··· WE MUST, **TOO!** WITHOUT *MERCY,* STAMP OUT OPPOSITION! NO NEW MOVEMENT HAS SUCCEEDED *USING MERCY* AND *MUSHY BROTHERHOOD!*

What? How about the early Christians?

COME NOW! DO YOU FORGET HOW THEY TREATED THOSE POOR LIONS?

VICKSBURG POST

THE S.S. PAT C.

120

A BACKWARD CONFRONTATION

Wherein we mind our queose and puce stamps ....

122

123

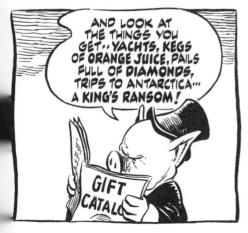

THE STAMP OF GENIUS

❦

Here we find the true color of their puce heartland …

WHAT?! FOR TWO MILLION STAMPS?

YOU'D HAVE THE CLEANEST TEETH IN TOWN FOR 268 YEARS.

Y'KNOW···· WHAT YOU **COULD** DO IS INVENT A TOOTHPASTE SAN'WICH·· *ANOTHER NATIONAL FIRST FOR OKEFENOKEE KNOW-HOW!*

WELL, YEAH·· THAT PLAN GOT A *LITTLE* MERIT····

A *LITTLE?! MAN!* DO YOU REALIZE YOU'D HAVE THE **FIRST** SAN'WICH WHAT WOULD BRUSH YOUR TEETH IN **TRANSIT?**

Y'KNOW, IF I HAD THE MONEY I'D BE A **RICH** MAN ON WHAT WE COULD GET FOR THESE **PUCE TRADING STAMPS.**

NO QUESTION·· IT HAPPENS I HAVE A TIDY SUM TUCKED AWAY.

HERE, WITH MY YO-YO, MY OUIJA BOARD, THE LOOSE JELLY, SECOND-HAND CHOON GUM, AN' MY **REVOLVER,** IS A PACKET OF BILLS THAT I ····

THIS IS A SMALL **FORTUNE** IN BILLS YOU GOT HERE, HOUN'DOG····

THE **LAST** OF THE BEAUREGARD FRONTENAC BUGLE-BOY III **BONANZA** OF STORIED FAME.

IT GOT A KINDA **FUNNY** LOOK.

FUNNY? IT'S **BEAUTIFUL** ··· YOU JUS' AIN'T USED TO SEEIN' FIFTY DOLLAR BILLS.

128

WE BEEN THINKIN' OF DOIN' BUSINESS IN THEM OL' PUCE STAMPS.

MR. PIG GAVE US THE GIFT CATALOG... *FULLA* STUFF.

HIM! CLAIMS WE DIN'T HIT THE MOON HARDLY ATALL... AFTER ALL THE MANY EXPERIMENTS US MICE WENT THRU...

WELL..MEBBE HE WASN'T *LOOKIN'* AT THE TIME... DIN'T *SEE IT.*

PHOO....THE OTHER FELLA WHAT WENT INTO ORBIT SAID *HE DIDN'T SEE NO ANGELS.*

THANKS

IS IT SO IMPORTANT FOR *YOU* TO SEE THE ANGELS? ALLUS THUNK IT WAS BETTER IF THE ANGELS KEPT A EYE ON *YOU*...

131

SPY ARE SQUARE

❦

To peer upon a friend is to make every friend a peer?

133

BET IT AIN'T NO PATCH ON WHAT HAPPENED WHEN I WAS A BOY... A DRUMMER LIVED IN OUR SPARE ROOM, DIN'T PAY HIS RENT AN' ONE NIGHT HE **SNUCK OUT** BY A ROPE LADDER.

DADDY LEANED OUT AN' **CUT THE ROPE**... THE DRUMMER LIT RUNNIN' AND TORE OFF INTO THE **NIGHT.** "THAT," SAID MAMA, "IS THE FASTEST TRAVELIN' ROOMER WE EVER HAD WITH US."

DON'T TELL ME THAT RUMOR... IT AIN'T POLITE TO LISTEN.

IN THAT CASE, D'YA MIND IF I JUS' TELLS IT?

OH, I GUESS NOT.. AIN'T NO HARM IN **TELLIN'**... JUS' IN **LISTENIN'** TO RUMORS.

WELL, MR. PIG AN' FIDO, THE LIBERATOR, IS AROUND TRYIN' TO PASS OFF **PUCE** TRADING STAMPS TO THE INNOCENTS.

HARD TO FIND **THEM TYPES,** THE INNOCENTS, I MEAN.

STEADY STEADY

SO FAR THEY FOUND CHURCHY AN' BEAUREGARD.. **THERE'S SOMETHIN' BEHIND ALL THIS!**

BUT I THOUGHT YOU WASN'T GONE TO LISTEN?

OH, I **AIN'T**... I'M JUST STUDYIN' THE SITUATION.

QUAIL FELLOW MELL WET

✳

Beneath the bushel all is bright...

Very jolly, meeting you two...

IS CHARMING!

My friend and I were wondering about your philosophy.

IS ROUGHLY: BE KIND, GENTLE, GENEROUS AND NEVER GIVE A SUCKER AN EVEN BREAK...

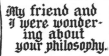

Brother!

IS PLEASURE!

YOUR FAMILY BEEN HERE LONG, FRIEND?

SI ... IS MOST EARLIEST SETTLERS...

BEFORE REVOLUTION! BEFORE FLAG! BEFORE MAYFLOWER!

WE'RE BLOOD BROTHERS... WHERE'S YOUR FEATHERS?

ME, I'M NO THE BIRD, SENOR.

137

WELL, I GOT NEWS... IT'S ON A *POSTCARD* WHICH I LOST, BUT I *RE*-MEMBERS IT.

WHUT'D SHE SAY?

IT WAS FROM A FAN... SAYS YOU'S "*ALWAYS IN THE MIDDLE* ... *YOU DON'T NEVER TAKE FIRM STANDS* ..." FROM A FELLOW NAME OF KELLY...

OOG! HIM!

NEVER MIND, TELL HIM, DID HE EVER SEE *TWO DOGS FIGHTIN'* OVER A BONE? HE'LL SAY, "YEH", THEN ASK, *DID HE EVER SEE THE ONE IN THE MIDDLE, THE BONE, FIGHT? HO HO?*

M?

S'POSE YOU GOT A *NUT* IN THE *MIDDLE*, RIGHT 'TWEEN THE JAWS OF A NUT-CRACKER? *EVER SEE THE NUT FIGHT BACK?*

MM...WHAT KIND OF NUT?

WHO IS HOO?

Stamp a grape and it comes down wine...

140

CHEESE KNEAD NEW NEED? *WHAT KIND* OF CHEESE DO YOU WANT HIM TO SAY?

ANY KIND!... SAY "CHEESE", KID.

LEIDERKRUNCH? CAMELBURT? ROCKFURT? BEL PIAZZA? TUTTI FRUTTI? GORGONDOLA? HEAD? JACK? POT? RAT?

HE AIN'T SMILIN' LIKE HE SHOULD.

HAM SANDWICH!

HIS FAVORITE CHEESE! A MASTER STROKE, CHIEF!

SNAP

PLOP

DOGSLIFE, THE MAGAZINE OF FASTER HORIZONS, SENDS DOUGHTY REPORTING TEAM TO PLUMB *SWAMP* STORY.

KEEP UP, KID, IF YOU WANNA BE IN THE PIX.

RESEARCH DEPARTMENT AUTHENTICATES CREATURE AS MARSUPIAL, POGO.... *HEY*, NOT SO FAST ON THE HORIZONS, CHUM.

AROOGAT! AROOGAT!

IT'S TEAM WORK ON THESE DEPTH STORIES THAT COUNTS, CRUCIBLE, MY BOY...

RIGHT, CHIEF!

BZM BZM BZM

DOGSLIFE! THE MAGAZINE OF DEPTH PERCEPTION, CRUCIBLE!

OH, IT'S DEEP, CHIEF!

SOMEHOW, THIS PART OF THE SWAMP *ALLUS* SCARES ME...

142

A SHORT 22

·→)|(←·

Wherein we look for the mother load of a fowling piece···

YOU RELIES ENTIRELY ON BETSY TO MAKE ALL JUDGEMENTS?

OL' BETSY HERE SPEAKS WITH A VOICE OF AUTHORITY, TURTLE.

THEY'S NO SECOND GUESSIN' WHEN OL' BETS DELIVERS A VERDICT.

BUT HASTY SHOOTIN' LIKE THAT···· DON'T YOU MISS OR MAKE MISTAKES?

MISS? *NEVER*··· 'COURSE, NOW AN' THEN I MIGHT MAKE A LI'L MISTAKE···

AFTER ALL, I AIN'T *COMPLETELY* PERFECT.

YOU GUYS OUGHT TO BE THANKFUL.

FER WHAT?

FER GUYS LIKE I WHAT'S WILLIN' TO TAKE THE LAW INTO OUR OWN HANDS···THE ORNERY CITIZEN GOT PROTECTION.

YOU KNOW YOU KIN GO FORWARD, CONFIDENT THAT US MI-NUTE MEN IS RIGHT BEHIND YOU···

YEH··· WITH A GUN.

DERN RIGHT!

TO SHOOT OR NOT

To shoot, we learn, is not the question.
To miss is the problem.

THE BUGS IN THE RUG

Here we learn to never let the
right hand know what the right
is doing ···

THEN, FINALLY, THEY FORGOT ALL 'BOUT WHAT THEY WAS S'POSE TO CELEBRATE SO EVER SINCE, THEY BEEN CELEBRATIN' CELEBRATION DAY.

LAND! YOU FIX ALL THESE FIXIN'S?

YEP... AN' IF I DOES A GOOD JOB THEY INVITES ME...

I BRUNG EVERYTHING FOR THE PICNIC 'CEPT THE SALT...

I'LL RUN OVER AN' GIT IT... YOU WATCH THE GRUB.

WHY DON'T BOTH OF YOU RUN OVER? WE'LL WATCH THE GRUB.

ANTS!

AT YOUR SERVICE...

THANKS... BUT CHURCHY WILL RUN HOME FOR THE SALT... I'LL STAY HERE AN' WATCH YOU.

USUALLY, IF ANYBODY SETS AROUND WATCHIN' ANTS, HE GETS A LI'L ACTION... BUT YOU IS PERTY QUIET...

YOU JUST WAIT...

LOOK!

LOOK

LOOK

LOOK

LOOK

LOOK

LOOK

GOTTA GIVE 'EM TIME FOR THIS, NOW...

SWISH

ALLUS BRING TWO CAKES TO A PICNIC.... ONE FER YOU AN' ONE FER UNEXPECTED COMPANY....

HE TOOK A LONG TIME LOOKIN' 'ROUND... S'POSE HE REALLY SAW SOMETHIN' PERTY GOOD?

GOOD! BRAND NEW CAKE! NOW I OUGHT TO MAKE A WELCOME SIGN....

LET'S SEE.... WELCOME, OKEFENOKEE GLEE 'N' PERLOO UNION.... MAN! THAT WON'T FIT....

BUT.... ABBREVIATION OUGHT TO FIX IT....

THERE....

WELCOME OGPU

WELCOME, OKEFENOKEE GLEE 'N' PERLOO UNION

WELCOME OGPU

GRASSHOPPLE, D'YOU MIND WATCHIN' THE STORE WHILST I TRAIP OFF AN' HELP **CHURCHY** FIND THE **SALT** FER THE **PICNIC**?

WHO'S THE PICNIC FOR?

FOR A BUNCH OF ANIMAL TYPES BELONG TO THE OKEFENOKEE GLEE AN' PERLOO UNION.... DON'T LET 'EM **TALK** YOU INTO ANYTHING.

THE BACK OF MY INSECK HAND TO 'EM!

I DON'T **BELIEVE** IN TALKIN' ANIMALS!

151

THE GRAND REUNION

❧ ✿ ❧

The super-duper market place...

153

I'LL PUFF GO WITH PUFF YOU PUFF...

WONDER WHAT THEY'S TALKIN' ABOUT? ALL THAT PUFFIN', MEBBE THEY'S A NEW **STEAM ENGINE** AT THE **FORT MUDGE** DEPOT.

WELL, I'D GIVE A PERTY TO SEE IT...

¡Quiero comer! ¡Tengo hambre!

WELCOM OGPU

LOOK! THE FEAST IS FOR US!

I THUNK YOU'D NEVER FIND THE SALT.

I DIN'T... SO I TOOK SUGAR INSTEAD.

155

ALL DRESSED UP

§

Wherein we learn there are plenty of places to go in case of fire...

158

159

HOW IT ALL STARTED

NOT ONLY THAT BUT THE INVENTION OF THE SEEGAR LED TO A LOT OF IMPORTANT *SCIENTERRIFIC* DISCOVERIES.

FACT?

FACT! Y'SEE, THE MAN WHAT TOOK THE V. P.'S ADVICE GOT HISSELF A EAR OF TOBACCO AN' ROLL 'EM UP LIKE A *HOT DOG*.

FACT?

FACT! SO ONCE HE GOT IT... *OH,* HE KNOW IT'S A SEEGAR ALRIGHT, BUT HE *DON'T* KNOW WHAT TO DO WITH IT... IT AIN'T GOOD TO *EAT*...

IT AIN'T GOOD TO *DRINK*...

SO HE ASK HIS WIFE AN' SHE SAY, "FOR ALL OF ME YOU KIN SET FIRE TO IT!" *WELL,* THIS WAS '*WAY* BACK AN' THE MAN SAY, "*FIRE!?* WHAT'S THAT?" SO HE DECIDED HE HAFTA INVENT *FIRE,* TOO!

HE GET A STICK AN' ROLL IT BACK AN' FORTH... SUDDENLY, THE LI'L TWIGS, ETC., CATCHES FIRE AN' THE MAN CALLED THE VEE-PEE ON THE PHONE AN' SAY, "*BOSS,* WE INVENTED FIRE!"

V. P. SAY, "WHAT WE GONE *DO* WITH IT?" MAN SAY, "WE GONNA LIGHT THEM *DAGNABBED SEEGARS* WITH IT!"

FACT?

FACT!

162

WILIER LIFE

¿

CHARLESTON! CHARLESTON! YAY BO! I LOVE MY WIFE BUT O.U. KID!

WHOA! WHOA!

ZAM! WATCH MY DUST! GET A HORSE!

THAT ALL WENT OUT WITH THE FLAPPER IN THE RACCOON COAT!

I KNOW... I WENT OUT WITH HER MYSELF.

SIGH

SHE WAS A VISION OF LOVELINESS ··· ULP!

HEY!

WHY, MIZ RACKETYCOON! YOU GIVED OL' CHURCHY A START.

HMMPH!

HE GONNA NEED ONE···· HE'S S'POSED TO BE BABY-SETTIN' MY TAD··· ME AN' THE MISTER IS ENTERED IN A ROCK AN' ROLL CONTEST THIS AFTERNOON.

RESEARCH ITEM NO. 1: Wildlife is changed.

164

165

THE BRAIN BURGLE

TODAY'S GUESS STAR

WRITE IS MIGHT

NEVER SAY DIE, I SAYS···CAST YOUR PEEKABOOZE ON **THAT!**

"On a day, alack the day! Love, whose month was ever May, Spied a blossom passing fair Playing in the wanton air-."
Shakespere
WHAT BOSH IS THIS?

SHE DON'T RHYME?

IT RHYMES! IT RHYMES! BUT WHAT **SENSE** DO IT MAKE?

I'LL GIVE IT **ANOTHER** WHACK.

WHENCE DO I GET SUCH FRIENDS?

HOW NOW?

GREAT! JUS' GREAT!
*"THE LITTLE FROG WAS COLORED PINK. WHAT DOES A PINKIE FROGGIE THINK? I'LL TELL YOU WHAT THE FROGGIE THUNK···
HE THUNK: KA·CHUNK KA·CHUNK KA·CHUNK···"*
SUPERB!

YOUR POEMS IS GIVED ME THE **BEST IDEA** IN A LONG BRILLIANT CAREER OF **SINGLE-HAND THINKIN'!**

NOW LISTEN AT WHAT YOU IS WROT···· **YOU** CAN'T READ THO' YOU CAN WRITE···· AN', BROTHER BEAR, YOU IS *TALENT!*
*"♪ HAVE **YOU** TRIED CRIPSEY CHOOLIE WUMMIES? THEY'RE COOL AND GLUE AND YUMMIES! THEY HOLD TOGETHER TUMMIES····SO GO AN' ASK YOUR MUMMIES FOR YUMMY YUMMY WUMMIES ···*
THEY'RE GRISTLE TO YOUR MILL!" ♪

STUFF LIKE THAT ON THE TEEVY WILL MAKE YOU A **MILLION.**

NO! NO! I CAN ALWAYS ROB GRAVES.

174

B.B.'S TEEVY COMMERCIALS NEED WHAT, TECHNICALLY, WE TEEVY PEOPLE CALL A WHAM OR BLAST ENDING.

RIGHT!

AN' I GOT ONE THAT IS THE UTTER OUTER END··· I'LL LAY THE EGGS OUT AN' WE'LL WATCH THEM HATCH INTO RUBIES.

ALL SET, A.A.! GIVE THE PROP A WHIRL AN' CLEAR THE RUNWAY.

OWL GOT A BIGGER WHAM ENDING THAN SHOOTIN' OFF A GUN, B.B.··· SING YOUR COMMERCIAL TO THE TUNE OF FRANKIE SCHUBERT'S UNFINISHED SYMPHONY.

♪ OH, A CHUMMY SIGHT IS A YUMMY BITE OF A WUMMIE···· OF A WUMMIE··· THEY'RE MADE OF GLUE, THEY STICK TO YOU AND YOUR TUMMY···AND YOUR TUMMY ♪

GO!

WHAM

NOW WHAT?

NOW HEAD FOR THE HILLS AFORE HE THINKS OF A WHAM ENDING OF HIS OWN.

ROWR!

MA BOONEY LICE SODA DEVOTION

181

182

Brain Washday

A INNERNATIONAL BRAIN TWISTER AN' *YOU* CLAIMS IT'S SIMPLE.... WHAT'S THE ANSWER?

THIS GUY WITH *TWO LEGS* GOT A *THREE-LEGGED* GIRL FRIEND...

AN' HE'S SITTIN' ON *HER* LAP.... HER BROTHER WHO GOT *ONE LEG*...

....IS SITTIN' ON *HIS* LAP .... ALONG COMES THE FATHER ... *HE GOT FOUR LEGS* ... HE GRAB UP THE ONE-LEGGED LI'L BOY AND *RUSH* HIM OFF TO BED ....

THE YOUNG MAN GET UP AN' THROW HIS THREE-LEGGED GIRL FRIEND AFTER THE *FOUR-LEGGED* FATHER ...

NO! NO! TWO LEGS IS A MAN SETTIN' ON A THREE-LEGGED STOOL, EATIN' A LEG OF MUTTON ... A DOG COMES BY AN' STEALS THE MUTTON .... THE MAN GETS UP AN' HE THROWS THE STOOL AT THE DOG ...

WHAT!?

HOW RIDICULOUS CAN YOU GET?

BAZZ FAZZ!

TWO CAN HIDE CHEAP AS ONE

186

THE NEW LOOK

I GOT A **GOOD MIND** TO GO BACK AN' GIVE 'EM A PIECE OF IT!

YOU WANT TO KNOW WHAT'S **WRONG** WITH THE **MODERN AMERICAN THEATRE?**

NO!

BROTHER, I GOTTA HAND IT TO **YOU**... NO WISHY-WASHY ANSWER FROM **YOU** WHEN A GENT ASKS A QUESTION.

NOSSIR! A MAN ASKS YOU, MAN-TO-MAN, EYE-TO-EYE, TOOTH-TO-TOOTH, "YOU WANT TO KNOW SOMETHIN'?" AN' DO YOU **HOLD BACK?**

NO... YOU'RE RIGHT AS RAIN.

I ASKS, **BOLD-LIKE,** DO YOU WANNA KNOW WHAT'S WRONG WITH THE AMERICAN THEATRE?

AN' I ANSWERS, **BOLD-LIKE, NO!**

GOOD... SO I'LL TELL YOU IN WORDS MORE PRICELESS THAN THE RHINESTONES OF KOHINOOR.

BUT, DEAR BOY, LET US NOT DISREGARD MY ATTITUDE... ONE IN WHICH I MUST COURTEOUSLY REFUSE AND SAY...

NO!

BUT THAT'S *EGG-ZACKLY* WHY I GOTTA TELL YOU... YOU'RE SO FIRM, SO FAIR, SO FRIENDLY...

SO FLEET OF FOOT.

THE THING THAT'S WRONG IS THEY DON'T USE FROGS LIKE THEY USED TO... THE COP USED TO SAY, *"HEAR THAT?"* AT THE START OF THE SCENE AND THE BUTLER WOULD SAY, "YES, I HEARD SOMEBODY *CROAK!"* KNOW WHO IT WAS? A *FROG!*

A UNION FROG! A ACTIN' AMPHIBIAN! THEY HAD FROGS ON THEIR UNIFORMS... THE ACTORS WERE CRAZY ABOUT FROGS... EVEN SHAKESPERE IN "OTHELLO" SAYS...

..."I HAD RATHER BE A TOAD AND LIVE UPON THE VAPOUR OF A DUNGEON..."

THAT'S "TOAD" NOT FROG!

GOSH... THAT'S RIGHT...

THAT'S *THE POINT*... YOU SEE, EVEN THE BARD DISCRIMINATED... WE HAVEN'T HAD ANY STEADY WORK SINCE 1612... *FROGS OF THE WORLD, ARISE!*

TAKE IT UP WITH EQUITY.

192

RETREAD TO HISTORY

CHEERFLE CHARFLE

196

197

CHEERFUL CAMP SIBERIA

200

TIME TO HEAD HOME!

OH, WHEN POOR POGO IS WRAPPIN' UP THE BLANKETS, TYIN' UP THE FIREWOOD...

"PACKIN' THE TENTS..."

"BUNDLIN' UP THE SLEEPIN' BAGS..."

"CLEANIN' THE POTS FOR THE LAST TIME..."

♪

CAMP SIBERIA

THEN, HE'LL BE SAD... BREAKIN' UP CAMP IS A SAD, SAD BUSINESS!

BUT... WHERE IS HE?

HE SNUCK OFF TO SAVE HIS HEART FROM BREAKIN'.

THE DOG!

BY DOG NAB! THERE'S GRATITUDE FOR YOU! MAKIN' US DO OUR OWN PACKIN'!

WHAT A INGRATE.

HOWDY

HOWDY

BOY! BOY! JUS' WAIT'LL NEXT YEAR!

UP IN THE AIR

RUN
RUN
RUN
RUN
RUN
RUN
(STUMBLE)
RUN
RUN
RUN
(GASP)

205

206

NO NOSE IS GOOD NOSE

NOSTRIL O'TOOLE···· THE OLFACTORY EXPERT, IS LOST HIS JOB!

WHOM IS THAT?

NOSTRIL O'TOOLE WAS HEAD BLOODHOUND AT THE PEN···· HE LOST HIS SENSE OF SMELL!

HEE YUCK A WOCK GOOKLE A RACK A RACK A WOOK!

OH, KIND-SIR, DO NOT GRIEVE SO···· DO NOT BE CARRIED AWAY, KIND-SIR, SIR!

HICK HOCK HOOK HICK HACK HUCK HICK HOOK

YOU GOT THE HICKORY-CUPS···

WHACK!

MAN! WHAT GUV ME THEM HINKUPS?

WHEN I TOLE YOU THE SAD NEWS···

208

"Y'KNOW, YOU DOGS MAKES A AWFUL BIG HOOT'N' HOWLER 'BOUT BEIN' DOGS! WHAT STUCK-UPS!"

"HA! THE VOICE OF A IGGER-NOMUS."

"TROUBLE WITH ALL YOU NON-DOGS, YOU AIN'T GOT NO BRINGIN' UP... YOU NEVER HAD NO ACTUAL REAL CHANCE."

"HOO! IT IS TO YAWN."

"YOU GOTTA ADMIT, AS MANY OF MY HIPSTER FRIENDS COMMENT, IT AIN'T EVERY CAT CAN BE A REAL DOG."

"HO! I WATCHED YOU LAS' WEEK, GRIEVIN' 'BOUT OL' NOSTRIL O'TOOLE, WHAT LOST HIS JOB AS HEAD BLOODHOUND... PHOO! ALL YOU DOGS DOES IS WHOOP AN' BARK AN' HOP-FROG AROUND LIKE UNTO A SQUIRRELED-BIRD! WHAT'S YOU DOGS GOT WHAT US OTHER HUMANS AIN'T?"

"A KEEN SENSE OF SMELL..."

"A KEEN SENSE OF SMELL? FOOF! HALF YOU GUYS COULDN'T SMELL YOUR WAY TO THE NUT-HATCH ON A COCOANUT BOAT."

"SIR!"

WELL, FOR A SAMPLE, US DOGS FOLLIES THE **THROWN OBJECT**···OUR KEEN NOSE TRACES THE BALL THRU THORN AN' THICKET.

NOTHIN' TO IT!

SMELL IT··· THEN WHEN I THROW IT, *TRACE IT!*

OOG!

SNERF

FETCH BOY!

AN' 'MEMBER TO THINK OF THE BALL AS SOME **DELICIOUS** GOODIE.

ARF

ARF! ARF! OH, MY! SUCH A **DELICIOUS** GOODIE··· I SHALL TAKE YOU HOME TO MY MASTER. GOODIE! GOODIE!

OH, SUCH A GOODIE! I SHALL SHARE IT WITH MY MASTER.

MY MASTER WILL PET ME AN' PAMPER ME···· *HEY!* WHERE IS THAT DAGNABBIN' DOG?

A DELICIOUS GOODIE, HUH? AARGH!

MY KEEN NOSE SMOLLED YOUR PICNIC LUNCH APPROACHIN' SO I SENT A **DOG FRIEND** AWAY TO PLAY WITH A BALL ···

PERHAPS IS GOOD···· THERE ONLY IS MUCH ENOUGH FOR THE TWO.

A MOOT SNOOT

212

KAKE KOOK KICKS

REAL LOW HI-BERNATZ

218

BEAU BUMMEL

PUTTIN' THE FOOT IN FOOTBALL

WHAT IN THE *WORLD.!?*

I IS DECIDED TO BECOME A *BIG TIME FOOTBALL PLAYER* AN' GIT *MY NAME* IN THE *PAPER.*

SON, YOU IS COME TO THE *RIGHT PLACE*··· I WAS ONCE THE *GREATEST BROKEN FIELD-RUNNER* OF *RICOCHET U.*

WHO BROKE YOU?

LEMME TAKE YOUR *FOOTBALL,* *POGO*··· I'LL SHOW YOU HOW I USE'TA *PIG* THE *BOOTSKIN*···

BUT·· BUT····

I MEAN *BOOT* THE *SKINPIG*··· THAT IS, *SKIN* THE *PIGBOOT*··UH··I····

BUT····

WELCOME TO *SCHOOL!* WELCOME WELCOME!

WELCOME YOURSELF, SPORT.

INSIDE JAB

225

THE STARE WAY
TO SUCCESS

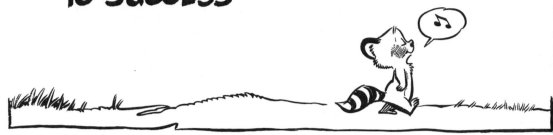

227

The JACK ACID SOCIETY BLACK BOOK

This book, such as it is, is for
Inky Blackman, newspaperman extraordinary,
who does not deviate.

INTRODUCTION

All of the right-wing societies which might be confused with the Jack Acid Society are understandably as nervous as a troop of elephants trying to walk on water. They claim to be apprehensive of the far left, the left and even the middle, but they also keep a sharp eye on each other.

There are too many saviors in the league. Each of them is sniffing the air, testing the surface and taking personal affront at all sudden noises. It is a thoroughly naïve reporter who will take one ultra group for another or claim that one is in sympathy with another. This easy identification as fellow travelers merely because they are all wandering the same bog is rightfully deplored by every crowd. A large part of this mutual distaste is economic in root. There is keen competition now, not only for the disciples, but for the contents of the collection plate.

There has also been a little God snatching and flag appropriating here and there. Most societies claim that God is on their side and, by implication, it is questionable whether He is on any other side. However, the Jack Acids were formed first, and first come is first served. If the flag and God belong to anyone, they belong to them.

It has been claimed by some that the Jack Acid Society is an imitation, in fact a parody, of extreme rightists. Nothing could be further from the truth. The student will find in the documents on display in this Black Book evidence that the main drive and spirit of the personalities involved have altered not one whit in many years. Other rightist groups have even insisted by mail (implying boycott and threat) that the members of the Jack Acid Society are copying their stuff and are caricatures of the "true" right-wing factions. The Jack Acids can only insist that the case is quite the other way around. The

Jack Acid Society was formed first, secretly, it is true, but spiritually open, honest and forthright.

Molester Mole is introduced here in a documentary picture history taken from the files of the Society. It can be seen that he is ever the same. Exactly that can be said for Deacon Mushrat. Again our worthy friend from the distinguished Mi-nute Man group is indistinguishable from many whom it has been our pleasure to have had in the organization for many years. A day-by-day account of an organizational attempt of recent months, reprinted here for the record, will be found to be very much like the activities of the Society in years past.

One of our men, the other day, was standing at a bar near (but NOT in) the United Nations Building. Our friend wondered idly what sort of hotel building the structures would make when the international organization had disbanded. His companion said: "Well, the reason to not like the World Organization is that it endangers the Federal Sovereign State; the reason to dislike the Federal Sovereign State is that it infringes upon the rights of the individual state in the U.S. family; the reason to be wary of the individual state is that it crimps the freedom of the city; the reason to fear the city's set of rules for order is that it cuts in on the activities of the citizen; the reason to suspect your neighbors' rights and prerogatives is that they MAY crowd yours. The only answer is to live alone."

Now this jokester may have thought he was funny, but the Jack Acid Society thoroughly endorses the final choice by Chicken Little in the poem which was in business a number of years ago. It follows, and shows clearly, that the quest for Safety was initiated NOT by Johnny-come-latelies but by the Jack Acids themselves.

The Prince of Pompadoodle
  Lived behind a castle wall,
Behind a moat, behind a guard
  Of twenty soldiers tall.

The Prince of Pompadoodle
  Was the safest man alive.
Each day he wrote how long he'd lived
  And multiplied by five.

The Prince of Pompadoodle
  Would survive, he did decide,
Five times as long as he had been
  Alive before he died.

The Prince of Pompadoodle
  Called in the castle sage
For his advice in this pursuit
  Of long and fulsome age.

The Prince of Pompadoodle
   Heard in horror from this friend
That somewhere in the palace
   Was a cur who'd seek his end!

The Prince of Pompadoodle
   Scarce could credit a belief
His years might soon be sneaked away
   By some ungrateful thief.

The Prince of Pompadoodle
   Sent his every friend away
And sat alone, safe, locked alive,
   To count another day.

The Prince of Pompadoodle
   May hoard each empty hour,
But none can know; no word comes from
   The silent stony tower ---

THE SONG OF THE MOLE

I love you slobs
   and I'll take charge
To save some
   who're sensible.
I'll handle prob-
   lems small or large-
Ly incom-
   prehensible.

Despite the wounds
   and every task
Very ree-
   prehensible,
I'll call the tunes
   if you'll not ask
Me to be
   responsible.

AN INTRODUCTION TO
AND ADVICE FROM
THE FLOUNDER

Seated on the platform with me today
is a noble, patriotic citizen whom it is
my great privilege to share this platform
with and to introduce to
all of you from this platform
at this time---

But before I present this distinguished citizen
on the platform here, just a few words to explain
why we are here fore-
gathered on this
particular occasion---
An occasion which
looms larger and
larger as we pause
to consider every,
yes, consideration ---

Now we know, of course, that these are the times that try men's souls and purses what with income taxes on the rise and the enemy lurking on our doorstep.

Why the foe does not lurk on its own doorstep is not for me to fathom, but clearly their freedoms are less than ours which we are losing day by day--- We must be alert, awake, aware, fully armed, able to go without eating, drinking, breathing---

OR THINKING!

A communist! A traitor! I accuse him of deliberately lurking in the chandelier-- on our very doorstep--- Out with him, the treasonable dog!

236

I'M SORRY, I SHALL HAVE TO POINT OUT THAT THE TRAITOR IS AN INSECT, A BUG, NOT A **DOG**··· WE MUST BE ACCURATE···

I haven't introduced you yet. How can you get into a discussion with the Chair? He's a dog and out he goes!

It should be pointed out that, whereas, the Chair agrees that anyone may hold an opinion different than the Chair's and, whereas, such a person is quite free to express such an opinion, the Chair reserves the right to throw the bum out.

Democracy works two ways, you know. This is a Republic -- let's keep it that way.

But let me repeat, we must be
fair-minded, gracious to all,
alert, aware, awake and firm
in dealing with the guilty,
that is, those people who,
because they are not aligned
with us, must be against us ···

For we must ever realize, in the words of that
immortal patriot whom I shall never forget,
Benjamin Franklin, or was it Washington? In his
words, this patriot said, "These are the times that
try men's souls."

THAT PATRIOT WAS NOT A PATRIOT FOR
WE HAD NO FORMAL COUNTRY AT THE TIME···
THE D.A.R. WAS UNFORMED, THE STEAM-
BOAT NOT YET INVENTED. NO INDEED,
THE MAN WAS NO
PATRIOT IN MY
SENSE OF THE
WORD. INDEED,
HE WAS A
TRAITOR TO
THE LAND OF HIS
BIRTH! THE
ENGLAND OF
GEORGE THIRD.

238

You realize, of course, that you are not yet on the program?

WELL, WHO'S THE FLOUNDER HERE, YOU OR ME? STOP HOGGING THE LIMELIGHT... WHERE'S YOUR CONCERN FOR COUNTRY, MOTHER AND FLAG?

Very well, then, I'll introduce you immediately whether the meeting suffers or not.

THE WORLD WAITS...

We come now, friends and fellow patriots, to an estimable part of the evening-- a time we have all looked forward to for some time---

YOU SAID IT!

The esteemed gentleman who has flounded this esteemed organization and who graces our esteemed platform---

239

It is a pleasure to present one who is so universally admired, admired by all, that is, who are right minded and, naturally, right thinking, and, of course, right hearted --- and right handed. It should be brought out at this point that the

right handed person is correct, natural and beloved by Providence --- It has occurred to some of us who keep our eyes open that there are entirely too many left handed people worming their way into positions of power. According to reliable research, nearly one out of two federal tax collectors is left handed, a percentage of better than fifty percent, or ---

CRACK!

FRIENDS, ALLOW ME TO INTRODUCE MYSELF ---

240

BORING WITHIN AND WITHOUT

The start's the thing,
    The song to sing
  Is not the end
        Nor yet the way.
The thing to sing
      Must be the start,
  So brave, so big,
        So shrewd, so smart.

TERMITE OR
NOT TERMITE

To be boring within
    And boring without
And boring again
    And boring about
Is boring indeed
    And boring in doubt
And the wood I would eat,
    As I bored 'neath the bed,
Would go very neat,
    Very straight to my head.

242

WELL, I WAS ONE OF A GROUP WANTED TO GET THE LAST FELLOW ELECTED AGAIN···

YOU WAS A····?

EXACTLY···· I WAS A THIRD TERMITE ··· THEY WAS TWO FELLOWS AHEAD OF ME··· AN' THE WAY THEY WORKED IN THAT LOBBY, THEY NEAR BRUNG THE HOUSE DOWN.

SO, MR. TERMITE, YOU IS NO LONGER WITH THE U.S. GUMMINT?

AS YOU KNOW, THEY THRUN OUT EVERY THIRD TERMITE.

BUT THERE'S A LOT OF ONE TERMITES AND SECOND TERMITES LEFT···

YEP, AN' A LOT OF INSECTS WHAT'S NO TERMITES EVEN ···· OH, I TELL YOU····

····IT'LL BE A LONG TIME AFORE THEY GET ALL THE BUGS OUT OF THE GUMMINT.

A LAUGH ALOOF ALAS

A douser of a wowser
    Is the rouser in the wry
And a trouser on a blouser
    Is enough to make you cry.

HURK HURK THE LURK

Lurks there the lark
with hark so deft
He never to himself
is left?

To search out the enemy-- to cleanse us of the *scum* that lies over our beauty-- to **bite** thru the dirt--- We'll make a *Black List!*

WHAT'S THE NAME OF THE SOCIETY?

The Jack Acid Society

NAMED AFTER MR. *ACID*?

Well, it wasn't named before him.

WHAT ABOUT THAT *LIST*? THE **BLACK LIST** YOU WAS GONE MAKE UP?

Exactly! It'll be the names of all dangerous liberals and other scum.

You can help--- You know a lot of simps who believe in World Brotherhood-- a lot of bleeding hearts--- Put down their names.

JUST THOSE I'M SURE OF.

Fine, fine, fine----you've seen the light!

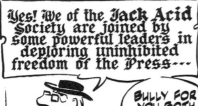

253

It's what we're against that's important --- For example, we, and others in high place, are against too much freedom --- People are too free with their speech.

THERE'S A DOCUMENT BEEN AROUND SAYS LIBERTY IS A RIGHT AN' THE GOVERNED GOT A RIGHT TO ALTER ANY GOVERNMENT WANTS TO DESTROY THE RIGHT.

Subversion! What's the document?

GUESS I LEFT MY COPY IN MY SUNDAY SUIT --- IT'S CALLED THE DECLARATION OF INDEPENDENCE.

Aren't you afraid to go out without it?

?

WHO'S IN THIS JACK ACID SOCIETY BESIDES YOU, DEACON?

An old colleague, writing in my newspaper under the name of Bobby Base.

Matter of fact, friend, I'm about to meet him now --- I've invited him to dinner --- keen mind, analytic eye --- never misses a thing --- Join us!

255

INDIAN SIGN

Which came first
    thru door ajar,
That Red Man or
    that D. A. R. ?

Oh, would a power the giftie gie us to see oursel's from afar...

WHAT'S THIS I HEAR 'BOUT MOLE AN' DEACON STARTIN' SOMETHIN' CALLED THE **JACK ACID SOCIETY** ···· AN' MAKIN' UP A **BLACK LIST**?

YEP···· THEY FIGGER **CIVILIZATION** IS GONE 'BOUT AS FAR AS JUPITER INTENDED···· THEY'S GONE GIT UP A LIST OF **ALL** WHO'S A ENEMY.

I GIVE 'EM THE **ONLY** NAME I IS **SURE** IS A ENEMY OF 'EM···· **ME**··· BUT I'M NOT SURE I MADE IT···· B'LEEVE I WAS **BLACKBALLED**.

TO BE **BLACKBALLED** FROM A **BLACK LIST** IS ALLUS BEEN MY AMBITION··· B'LEEVE I'LL VOLUNTEER **MYSELF**.

257

THE UNORIGINAL ABORIGINALS

We're surely best
    And not the worst,
Gee-ronimo!
      We got here first.

264

TO SUPERCEDE THE SUPER SEED

The growing up is only half,
    The growing down is sound;
So while your head is in the clouds,
    Your feet are on the ground.

POGO, THIS **NEWSPAPER** PUT OUT BY OL' DEACON POINTS OUT VERY CLEAR THAT THE **JACK ACID** SOCIETY, COMPOSED OF BONA FIDE INDIANS, HAS PUT ITS FINGER ON THE **PROBLEM**.

PROBLEM?

YESSIR···FOR ONCE HE SOUNDS RIGHT··· THE PROBLEM IS WE HAVE TOO MANY **NEWCOMERS**.

NEWCOMERS?

DANGEROUS NEWCOMERS.

LIKE **WHO?**

WELL, HE STARTS OFF WITH THE PASSENGER LIST OF THE **MAYFLOWER**.

AN' HE'S RIGHT... THE 'MERICAN INDIANS SHOULDA SPOKE UP *LONG AGO!*

DON'T YOU REALIZE THE MOLE AN' DEACON CLAIMS TO BE INDIANS ONLY FOR A REASON?

WELL, MAYBE IT'S A GOOD ONE.

THEY CLAIMS EVERYBODY WHAT'S NOT A ORIGINAL CITIZEN IS DANGEROUS... SO THEY IS BEIN' *INDIANS*...

WELL, THAT'S PERTY ORIGINAL...

YUP... THAT MAKES 'EM THE *MOST* ORIGINAL... THEREFORE, THE ONLY *CLEAN* CITIZENS.

WHO KNOWS...? MAYBE WE OUGHT TO *JOIN* 'EM.

AFTER ALL, THEY MAY BE *BORNE OUT.*

LIKE ON THEIR SHIELDS?

YOU MEAN THESE BOYS IS *COPS?*

266

MAN! IS YOU HEARD 'BOUT MOLE AND DEACON? *THEY* FORMED SOMETHIN' CALLED THE *JACK ACID* SOCIETY... A SNOOP GROUP!

AN' THEY'S INDIANS.

INDIANS!? THEM TWO CAN'T EVEN GROW FEATHERS.

THAT'S SO THEY CAN CLAIM THEY'S ORIGINAL CITIZENS.

CITIZENS!? THEY HAVEN'T EVEN VOTED 'TIL YET.

OH, I'D GIVE 'EM A PIECE OF MY MIND IF I COULD FIND IT... I MEANS, *THEM*.

Y'KNOW, OL' ALBERT LEADS A LIFE OF *NOISY DESPERATION*.

HOW BASE THE BALL

The basest ball
Of all the game
Is one that travels hence,
O'er our grass and our gloves
And finely, loves,
The fence.

CHICKEN LITTLE IS THE PITCHER AN' THE UMPIRE. HE CALLS 'EM AS HE SEES 'EM. HE SAYS HE WOULDN'T GIVE HIS **OWN** BROTHER A BREAK.

WHO'S HIS BROTHER?

HIS BROTHER IS **HERMAN**, THE HALF-HATCHED EGG OUT THERE ... HE'S THE **BALL**.

OL' HERMAN, THE HALF-HATCHED CHICK THERE, IS THE **KEY PLAYER** IN THE GAME...

AN' HIM SO **YOUNG!** MY, MY!

YEP... BUT HE GETTIN' TIRED OF THEM OTHERS ARGUIN'... THE **UMPIRE**, WHO IS THE **PITCHER**, WOULD THROW THE **BATTER** OUT OF THE GAME EXCEPT HE'S ALSO THE **CATCHER**.

WELL... THERE GOES THE BALL GAME!

HUH...? **I** DIN'T SEE **NOTHIN'**... SOMEBODY MAKE A PLAY?

NO... THE BALL GOT SORE AN' IS TAKIN' HIS-SELF HOME.

GOOD THING! **I'M** OUT OF POP-CORN.

274

THE OPEN-HEARTED MIND

We must not quiver,
Flinch or quail,
Shake or shiver,
Flunk or fail;
We all cheer them
big three R's,
Rudiment'ry one point stars.

THOSE PRINCIPLES WHICH, THROUGH PROPER POLLING, PROVE THEY ARE **GENERALLY,** IF NOT **UNANIMOUSLY,** ACCEPTABLE.

eh?

NOW GO FORTH AND BOYCOTT ALL ENEMY BUSINESS MEN.

Moomph moomph-- The Mole is right-- Support that which is estimated to be generally acceptable!

VIOLETS?

WHO WILL HAVE MY VIOLETS?

Hah-- selling violets at **your** age---How much do you intend to cheat me for?

OH----UH---- NOT VERY MUCH----

That's it! You young generation-- always willing to take advantage ----How much? Not that I intend to **purchase.**

I'M GIVIN' 'EM AWAY ----THEY'RE **YOURS.**

Hah! What? What's wrong with them?

UP THE REPUBLIC!

Oh, dig my shelter
Both wide and deep
As helter skelter
We dash to sleep.

280

282

I HEARS YOU TURNED OUR VOLUNTEER **BLACK LIST** OVER TO THE JACK ACID SOCIETY... YOU TRYIN' TO POKE FUN AT 'EM?

'COURSE NOT... I JUST WANT 'EM TO KNOW WE ALL GOT OUR OWN WAY OF VIEWIN' **OUR COUNTRY**... THEY GOT A RIGHT TO B'LEEVE THE WAY THEY DO ...**BUT**...

OL' KEN CRAWFORD

EVER'BODY GOT THEIR OWN WAY OF LOOKIN' AT **ANYTHING** ... DIN'T YOU EVER HEAR THE STORY OF THE BLIND MEN AN' THE ELEPHANT? ... EACH ONE WAS **PARTLY RIGHT.**

YEAH... AN' EACH WAS MOSTLY **WRONG** ... BUT YOU GOTTA REMEMBER EACH WAS **ALL** BLIND.

WASH. D.C.

THE S.S. KENNETH G.

THE TROUBLE WITH PEOPLE
IS PEOPLE

If we could climb
    the highest steeple
And look around at
    all the people,
And shoot the ones
    not wholly good
As we, like noble
    shooters, should,
Why, then there'd be
    an only worry···
Who would there be left
    to bury
    us?

285

BITTER, BITTER, DANKE SCHÖN

Bitter, sober, second thought,
    Of the things that we ought
To have done, is all for naught,
    For time that's gone can't be bought.

288

π IN THE SKY

It is no boon
   To hit the moon
With 100 megatons
   When, with some more,
We raise the score
   And hit 100,000 suns.

WHAT'S ALL THIS I HEAR ABOUT A **POPULATION EXPLOSION** DESTROYIN' EVERYTHING?

MAYBE NOT... THE AUTHORITIES HAVE A **CLEAN BOMB** NOW.

HUH? A **CLEAN** POPULATION EXPLOSION?

YES..A **NEUTRON JOB**....VERY SAFE FOR REAL ESTATE.

YOU MEAN THE NEW BOMB SPARES **BUILDINGS?** I DON'T OWN NONE!

HURRY OUT AN' BUY THE EMPIRE STATE OR SOMETHING.

BUT WHAT'LL HAPPEN TO **ME?**

OH, THE BOMB JUST KNOCKS OFF **LIFE**... YOU'LL BE GONE BUT THINK OF HAVIN' A ONE HUNDRED AN' TWO STOREY HEADSTONE.

BLACKLIST TO STARBOARD

The attrition of suspicion
Is a mission of the mind
That's built into a prison
With precision of a kind.

THE WAY YOU *JUMPS* REMINDS ME OF SOMETHIN'.

I'VE BEEN GOING OVER THESE NAMES ON THE BLACK LIST OF SIMPS.

AND, LOOK, THE ONLY NAMES IN THE SWAMP WHICH ARE MISSING ARE *YOU*, *ME*, WILEY CATT, SARCOPHAGUS MACABRE AND THE *TWO COWBIRDS*.

But the cowbirds are *known* Communists— They should be there.

TUT TUT... YOU FORGET THIS LIST IS FOR *ONE* PURPOSE...

WE WANT ONLY THOSE WE *SUSPECT*... ANYONE CAN BLACKLIST THE *KNOWN* ENEMY ... IT'S MORE SPORTING TO LEAVE *SOMETHING* UP TO *CHANCE*.

eh?

295

296

Black, black, black
Is the color of
My true love's heart.

SO OL' MOLE IS MAKIN' A BLACK LIST OF SUSPECTS *ONLY?*

HE CLAIM IT'S ONLY *FAIR*···NO SENSE PUTTIN' DOWN A NAME IF IT'S A *REAL SPY'S.*

BUT S'POSE HE MAKES *INNOCENT* PEOPLE SUFFER? *THAT'S NO GOOD.*

HE SAYS IT'S A *CHANCEY* WORLD.

AN' SO THAT'S THE CHANCE SOME PEOPLE GOTTA TAKE JUS' FOR BEIN' *INNOCENT*··· GIT PUT ON LIST OF *SUSPECTS.*

MOLE CLAIM *THAT'S NOT THE TOUGH CHANCE.*

HUH?

MOLESTER SAY *HE'S* THE *DARING* ONE··· EACH INNOCENT MAN IS TAKIN' ONLY *ONE* CHANCE···· BUT MOLE'S TAKIN' *HUNDERDS* OF CHANCES PUTTIN' THESE NAMES DOWN.

HE *SURE* IS··· 'SPECIALLY IF ALL OF 'EM GO SEE HIM AT ONCE.

299

HOW RAW THE RUE

How rueful, how doleful
    Is all of my crime,
For the thing I've been caught at
    Is not worth a dime.

Oh, I fear my career
    As a thief and a sneak
Has foundered upon a mole-
    Hill of a peak.

Listen, dear children,
    Be you brutish or prig,
Be caught not for peanuts
    Less the peanut is big.

303

PITY HE CAN'T BE ON IT HISSELF... EVEN **DEACON** MADE IT... DID YOU NOTICE....? TOO BAD MOLÉ IS LEFT OUT.

?

WELL, ANYWAY, **WE'RE** IN... IT'S NICE TO **BELONG**... NICE TO BE PART OF THE GROUP.

SNF

THE COWBIRDS ARE **RIGHT**... THE BLACK LIST INCLUDES EVERYBODY BUT **ME**... I'M THE ONLY ONE NOT SUSPECTED OF SOMETHING ... **ME**, LEFT OUT!

ARE YOU SURE YOU DON'T SUSPECT ME OF ANYTHING?

My esteem for you has never been more higher.

THERE'S A **NUMBER OF** THINGS I COULD... UH... SUGGEST...

You would never convince me---I have the utmost faith in your integrity--

WHY DO YOU **HATE** ME SO?

POMPETY POMP

There was one time
        a King of France
Who clad himself
        in brassy pants---
Pomp pomp a doodle
        pomp pomp!
Marched up the hill
        with all his men
And then he marched
        them down again---
Pomp pomp a doodle
        pomp pomp!

A MĬ-NUTE MAN'S CODE

LOT OF PEOPLE COME TO ME AN' SAY, "HOW COME YOU GUYS ARE ALL GEARED UP WITH **GUNS** AN' **AMMO** AN' TWO-WAY RADIO WHEN WE'RE PAYIN' GUYS TO DO IT?"

THEY GOT A POINT, THEM GOOD FOLKS THAT BEEN **PAYIN' TAXES** TO SUPPORT WHAT IS ACTUALLY A BUNCH OF KIDS PLAYIN' SOLDIER WHEN RIGHT IN THE GRASS ROOTS OF OUR COUNTRY WE GOT ABLE MEN THAT CAN SHOOT STRAIGHT...

WHAT DO **YOU** WANT PROTECTIN' THIS **PRECIOUS**, NOW, **HERITAGE**, *KIDS* OR *MEN* WHAT KNOWS WHAT THEY'RE FIGHTIN' FOR AN' DON'T GOTTA GUESS WHO THEY'RE FIGHTIN' LIKE KIDS DO?

EVER SINCE THEY BEEN
BUTTONIN' UP THE LIP
OF THEM IN THE KNOW
WHAT CAN TELL OUR
BOYS WHO EXACTLY IS
THE ENEMY, IT'S BEEN
UP TO US **PRIVATE CITIZENS**
AN' **PATRIOTS** TO FERRET
OUT THE **NO-GOODS** THAT'S
SUCH A CLEAR AND PRESENT
DANGER TO US ALL.

IT'S PEOPLE LIKE ME
WHAT COME FROM OLD
STOCK THAT KNOWS A
REAL AMERICAN FROM
A **PHONY** ··· THAT'S WHERE
THE GOVERNMENT BREAKS
DOWN ··· THEY GOT TOO
MANY CARD-CARRYIN'
SPIES FEEDIN' OFF **OUR**
TAX MONEY.

FOR **MY** DOUGH YOU GOT
TO HAVE A CLEAR EYE AN'
BE ABLE TO JUDGE A
MAN AN' NOT NO BUNCH
OF PAPER WORK AN' THEM
AFTERDAVITS ABOUT A GUY'S
HISTORY ··· IF HE DON'T HAVE
A **CLEAN LOOK** HE AIN'T GOT
NO CLEAN BILL OF HEALTH
IN **MY** BOOK.

LOT OF THEM DOPES IN HIGH PLACES MAYBE AIN'T DISLOYAL BUT, LIKE I SAY, THEY'RE DOPES AN' SWALLOW ALL THAT HOG-WASH ABOUT BROTHERLY LOVE AN' FORGIVENESS. THE **GOD** IN *MY* BIBLE IS **A GOD OF WRATH** AN' THAT'S WHOSE SIDE *I'M* ON!

WHAT YOU DO WITH GUYS LIKE THEM, THAT'S AGAINST *I* AN' **GOD**, IS LUMP 'EM ALL TOGETHER AN' GET RID OF 'EM ··· YOU DON'T GIVE 'EM ANY TRIAL. THAT'S WHERE WE ALWAYS MAKE A MISTAKE ···

WE TREAT THESE CRAVEN PUNKS AS IF THEY WERE DECENT MEN ··· SURE, MAYBE THEY DON'T **MEAN** HARM, BUT YOU GOTTA REMEMBER, LIKE I ALREADY POINTED OUT, THEY'RE PROVEN CRAVEN PUNKS THAT'S AGAINST GOD AN' SO *KNOCK 'EM OFF!*

JUST A MINUTE, FOLKS, I GOT A **TELEPHONE REPORT** HERE AT MY STATION THAT SOME **ENEMY INFILTRATOR** IS SNEAKIN' ACROSS MY **TERRITORY** JUST OFF OUR LEFT HERE ... I THINK I SEE THE NO-GOOD RAT ...

YEP ... THAT'S HIM **THERE** ... GOT HIM IN MY SIGHTS ... WAIT'LL HE'S IN THE **CLEAR** ... I'M LEADIN' HIM NOW, FOLKS ... HE WON'T GET AWAY WITH THIS ... STEADY ... STEADY ...

POW!

HELLO ... WHAT'S THAT, HARRY? I HIT **HERMAN?** OUR CAPTAIN? **DONE FOR?** GOT HIM RIGHT THROUGH THE NEW JACKET WE PRESENTED?

FOLKS, EXCUSE ME ... I GOT TO GO TO A **UNEXPECTED** PATRIOTIC FUNERAL.

ROOTY TOOT

The rooty toot toot
of the very
mī - nute,
The booty boot boot
of the band,
The cutey cute cute
of the less than
astute
Shivers and shudders
the land ---

HAYFOOT-STRAWFOOT
A FIRESIDE CHAT

MANY OF MY LETTERS, MUCH OF MY MAIL, AS A MATTER OF FACT, AND, IN FACT, A GOOD **PERCENTAGE** OF ALL THE INQUIRIES WHICH COME MY WAY ARE DIRECTED TOWARD THE QUESTION OF JUST WHAT IS OUR **POSITION** IN THE POLITICAL SCHEME ··· AS I UNDERSTAND THESE QUESTIONS THEY PERTAIN TO WHERE EXACTLY DO WE STAND POLITICALLY. RATHER THAN, HEH HEH, *PHYSICALLY* ···

THEY COULD, **OF COURSE,** HEH HEH, BE CONCERNED ABOUT JUST WHAT POSITION DO WE NORMALLY ASSUME. THEY **MAY** BE ASKING IF WE ARE **CROUCHED, STOOPED, ASKEW, OR SUPINE** ·· HEH HEH ··· (AND I MIGHT ADD AS AN ASIDE HERE TO POINT OUT THAT THE ABOVE SHOWS I HAVE **GENIAL** CHARM AND A SENSE OF HUMOR NOT **USUALLY** ASCRIBED TO ME ··· HEH HEH ···)

YES, WELL, TO CONTINUE ···

WE ARE HAPPY TO ANNOUNCE THAT OUR POSITION, THE POSITION OF THE **JACK ACID SOCIETY**, STANDS ERECT AND PROUD BEFORE FRIEND AND FOE. IN OTHER WORDS, WE ARE FOR THE **RIGHT**, ALTHOUGH THIS IS NOT TO CONFUSE OUR POSITION WITH THE FALSE POSTURING OF OTHERS.

THERE ARE SOME WHO SAIL UNDER FALSE COLORS CLAIMING THEY ALONE REPRESENT PATRIOTISM, MOTHER, COUNTRY, FLAG, CHURCH···· WELL, THEY **ALL** ARE UNDOUBTEDLY SUBVERSIVE ···· OUT TO DESTROY WE WHO TRULY BELIEVE ····

AS FAR AS THE EYE CAN REACH LIE THE PEACEFUL AND BEAUTIFUL THINGS WE BELIEVE IN, OUR HERITAGE: LIMOUSINES, COUNTRY ESTATES, MINKS. OTHERS DO NOT BELIEVE IN THESE PATRIOTIC THINGS ···· OTHERWISE THEY WOULD NOT BE BORING FROM WITHIN, UPHOLDING THE CONSTITUTION, MILKING WE HONEST TAXPAYERS OF OUR GOD·GIVEN SPOILS···· THAT IS, HARD·EARNED PITTANCES.

AS IS GENERALLY KNOWN,
WE ARE ON GOD'S SIDE
AND ALL WHO OPPOSE *US*
ARE AGAINST *GOD!*
···NOW, LET ME MAKE IT
QUITE CLEAR, WHEN YOU
PICK ON *GOD*, YOU PICK ON
ME! IT'S THE SAME THING
AS PICKING ON THE FLAG,
ALMOST; ··· GOD IS LIKE
THAT TO ME, KIND OF LIKE
A BROTHER, SORT OF ··· YOU KNOW ··· PRACTICALLY
ONE OF THE FAMILY.

DEFY US, DISAGREE WITH
US, IF YOU WILL ··· WE WILL
DEMOCRATICALLY THROW
YOU OUT OF THE GROUP···
YOU'LL BE ON YOUR OWN,
WITHOUT GOD ··· WITHOUT
THE FLAG ···EVEN WITHOUT
ME ··· YOU'LL HAVE ONLY
YOURSELF TO THANK FOR
SUCH A CALAMITY ···

NOW, SOME TEND TO CONFUSE
US WITH THE OPPOSITION IN
OUR TACTICS ··· NOTHING COULD
BE FURTHER FROM THE TRUTH···
IT IS NOT THE ENEMY
WITH THE BOMB WHO IS
THE MOST DANGEROUS ··· IT
IS THE TRAITOR IN OUR
MIDST··· *STOP THAT COUGHING
OUT THERE! IT IS A
TYPICAL COMMUNIST
TRICK!*

316

CROUCH NEARER TO THE **FIRE** HERE AND LET ME DELINEATE ON THIS **PINE SHOVEL** JUST HOW ONE SUPPOSEDLY TRUE CONSERVATIVE CLAIMED THAT **POLITICAL DIRECTION** AND **POSITION** HAVE SWITCHED ··· SUPPOSE ONE HAD BEEN ON THE **LEFT** OF THE ROAD ··· WELL, YOU MUST BEAR IN MIND THE ROAD HAS SHIFTED OVER.

THUS, ACCORDING TO THIS FELLOW, THE NEW ROAD GOES THRU HIS **OLD** POSITION ··· HE'S IN THE **MIDDLE** NOW. **OKAY,** SUPPOSE HE USED TO BE *RIGHT* OF CENTER ··· THE ROAD GOES THE **OTHER WAY** FOR THE CONSERVATIVE, *RIGHT?*

AND THE **RIGHT SIDE** OF *THAT* OLD ROAD IS THE **LEFT** SIDE OF THE SAME OLD ROAD GOING THE OTHER WAY ··· SO YOU FIND WHEN THE ROAD SHIFTS TO ITS **RIGHT** IT GOES THRU THE **LEFT** SPOT OR ITS **OLD** RIGHT SPOT MAKING *THAT* THE MIDDLE OF THE ROAD, TOO ··· **UNDERSTAND?**

317

318

THE CONTUSION OF CONCLUSION...

HERE ARE appended a few letters taken at random from the mailbag:

DEAR POGO:

It has never seemed to me that God promised to love just certain snobs and to leave out all non-members.

As ever,
WFS

DEAR POGO:

A long time ago, while Hitler was marching into the Sudetenland, I asked a fellow artist what he thought was the essential difference between communism and fascism. He was immediately aghast. People were easily taken aghast in those days. He explained that in the communist state, the state was for the individual, while in the fascist state, the individual was for the state. He seemed to think this explained everything until I asked him which individual the communist state was for. At this he grew sullen, and I did not finish the course. The same question to a man of different stripe brought the answer that of course fascism was very great because it meant that a great many sticks bound together produced strength. When I said that the key word seemed to be "bound," he, too, grew restive and denied me further enlightenment.

To me, totalitarianism remains totalitarianism. It is the same bomb, sometimes packaged one way, sometimes another.

Regards,
O.V.B.

DEAR POGO:

What a possum does is climb a tree and get himself out on a limb when he feels threatened. Then he's helpless perhaps, but he's not really hiding. A lot of people say that he also feigns death in such cases, but take it from me, he feigns death only when he is sure he *will* be dead if he doesn't.

Possums are very primitive Americans and have not learned very much in the 2,000,000 years they have been in this country. Even all that length of time as residents does not completely qualify them for the accolade of "native." A good many people think of them as something exotic, from South America, or Australia. That's because possums are marsupials and are not like the regular club members. In other words, they are different, and naturally are to be viewed with suspicion.

A good many people also think that a possum is ugly. But many prominent possums think that many other possums are beautiful. This sentiment accounts for a fairly high birth rate, which is deplored by non-possums but which has the solid backing of regular paid-up possums.

It is possible that the possum could have tried to emulate the lemming at one point and put out to sea in an attempt to find a marsupial paradise. But, as I say, he has not learned very much. This is his home country. He knows it and he loves it. He has never had to join anything except the United States of America. Although he may not feel that he is welcomed by the recent arrivals, the mammals—wolves, rats, bears, wildcats and other varmints—he is nonetheless *here*.

And *here* he *will* stay, out on a limb a good part of the time, looking innocent and surviving.

Yours,
FELLOW POSSUM